The Church and the World

To Benedict Groeschel, CFR
selfless servant, wise counsel.

The Church and the World

Essays Catholic and Contemporary

John Haldane

GRACEWING

Freedom Publishing
AUSTRALIA

First published in 2008

Gracewing
2 Southern Avenue, Leominster
Herefordshire HR6 0QF

in Australia by:
Freedom Publishing Pty Ltd
582 Queensberry Street
North Melbourne
Victoria 3051

Cover photo by *L'Osservatore Romano*

ISBN 978 0 85244 588 4

Typeset by Action Publishing Technology Ltd,
Gloucester GL1 5SR

Printed in England by
Athenaeum Press Ltd, Gateshead NE11 0PZ

Contents

Preface

The following pages contain a series of essays on a range of topics gathered within several sections. The connections between them are various. Some discuss particular individuals, such as the late Pope John Paul II and his successor Pope Benedict XVI, dealing with them as subjects of study in their own right, but they also recur elsewhere in the context of discussing various ideas or values. Some chapters explore large general issues such as faith and reason, evolution, humanism, and art; others focus on particular events such as the death of John Paul II and the papal conclave that followed it.

The connections between the essays crisscross in ways that mean that readers will find themselves returning to certain ideas or figures, or discerning parallels or analogies. It is also the case that while I have organised the various discussions within sections, and ordered the sections according to my own sense of how they might most interestingly proceed, it is possible for the reader to start with any section and read thereafter in any sequence of sections without facing the problem of having various sets of ideas presumed to have been previously read and reflected upon.

The essays are also generally fairly short. That is owing to the fact that most of them originated in pieces of writing done for newspapers and magazines. But all have been re-written to some degree or other, and often expanded. Nonetheless I have retained the essay form in the belief that this is an appealing and effective genre for raising issues for consideration. Readers can pick up the book with fifteen or twenty minutes to hand and begin and end a discussion. If they have time and are engaged they can continue again starting and ending an essay. In this way I hope they will see the volume as a resource for their own thinking, and, I hope, for discussion with others.

Besides the various topical and thematic connections there are a couple of other features that serve to unify the book. First and most obviously the outlook represented here is that of Roman Catholicism. It is not just that I discuss Catholic figures and subjects, but that I discuss them, and other issues, from a Catholic perspective. In some cases Catholicism is hardly if ever mentioned but what is under examination has been selected out of Catholic interest, is seen through Catholic lenses, and is thought about by a Catholic mind. That fact notwithstanding, indeed because of it, I would hope that this book might also be of interest to non-Roman Christians, to non-Christian believers, and to non-believing but curious agnostic and atheist readers.

These days it is common to see the term 'Catholic' qualified by 'liberal' or 'conservative'. I resist such terminology not just because I think it oversimplifies and misleads in the usual way of such terms when applied to characterise the viewpoints of mature and thoughtful people, but because they commit a category error. The terms 'liberal' and 'conservative' are political ones, not in the party sense necessarily, but in a broader political meaning. The other pair of terms less frequently applied in general journalism and commentary, but commonly used in religious reportage, namely 'progressive' and 'traditionalist' are, properly speaking, cultural labels.

The theologically relevant contrast is not that of political orientation or cultural sensibility, but instead one focused on belief and associated religious practice. It is the contrast between orthodoxy and heterodoxy; that is to say between adherence to and departure from the beliefs taught and accepted by the Church. While it would not be accurate to describe my religious outlook as conservative or traditionalist, nor as liberal or progressive, for these are crude oppositions generally lazily applied, it would be generally appropriate to describe it as 'orthodox'. This outlook informs the essays even when they are not explicitly concerned with doctrine, as they very rarely are.

The second unifying feature comes from the fact that I am a professional philosopher. For although these are not philosophical essays they do bear the mark of habits of philosophical thinking: the tendency to look for and to draw distinctions, to disambiguate, to be concerned with conceptual aspects of issues, to look for arguments and to assess their validity and soundness, and so on. Readers will find these habits being exercised even when the subjects under discussion are recent events, or works of art, and I hope they will find them helpful.

Lastly I should make clear that while I hold a position as a Consultor to a Pontifical Council (a Vatican department) namely that of Culture, the views developed here are my own and I do not write in any official capacity or with a view to representing any Vatican interest.

John Haldane
St Andrews

Acknowledgements

Most of the following chapters originate in whole or in part in articles first published in a range of newspapers and journals. All have been modified or expanded to some degree. The original sources are indicated as follows, and I am grateful to the various editors for permission to re-use material here.

1. 'Waiting in hope' first appeared as 'The Waiting Game', *Tablet*, 5 February 2005.
2. 'A Church and its critics' draws from 'Denunciations of Catholic Teachings', *Herald*, 6 November 1999.
3. 'Catholicism in an age of liberalism' draws from an article of the same title in *Priests and People*, May 1996.
4. 'Taking faith seriously' is based on 'Society has changed – not Catholicism', *Scotsman*, 8 June 2007, and 'No abstract dilemma', *Tablet*, 24 April 2004.
5. 'Sectarianism and culture' is based on 'The Case of Scotland's Shame', *Crisis*, January 2001.
6. 'The death of a prophet and the life of a saint' draws upon 'Closing Comments' and 'Canonisation will be a lasting memorial', *Scotsman*, 2 and 5 April 2005.
7. 'Where to now for the pilgrim church?' draws upon 'The Creation', *Sunday Herald*, 10 April 2005.
8. 'Gentle man who will rule by the book' is based on an article of the same title from the *Scotsman*, 21 April 2005.

9. 'Street fighter for God', is based on 'Thomas Winning: Street Fighter for God', *Tablet*, 23 June 2001.

10. 'Three nineteenth-century liberals' draws from 'Still guided by shining lights of the nineteenth century', *Scotsman*, 18 September 2006 and 'Ozanam's Society', *Scottish Catholic Observer*, 25 May 2007.

11. 'Philosophy in the life of the Church' is from A. Ivereigh (ed.), *Unfinished Journey: The Church 40 Years after Vatican II* (London, Continuum, 2003).

12. 'Religion, philosophy and faith' draws upon 'The proof is out there', *Catholic Herald*, 20 September 1996.

13. 'Who's afraid of evolution?' draws upon 'Creationism has its place, but not in science class', *Scotsman*, 22 March 2006, and 'Benedict XVI takes up the challenge of "evolutionism"', *Catholic Herald*, 20 April 2007.

14. 'The Church cannot do without intellectuals' is based on an article of the same title from *Catholic Herald*, 14 October 2005, and 'Whither British Catholic Culture?' *Catholic Times*, 22 July 2007.

15. 'Europe and the future of Christian humanism' draws from 'Making Europe Christian–Again?', *Catholic Herald*, 25 July 1997, and 'A New Humanism for Europe', an address to an audience of university professors meeting in Rome in June 2007.

16. 'More ethics, less emotion' draws material from an article of the same title published in the *Tablet*, 2 April 2005.

17. 'Sexuality, ethics and politics' draws from 'Questions of justice and morality', *Herald*, 22 January 2000, and 'The sexual politics we need', *Tablet*, 12 February 2000.

18. 'Scandal in the American Church' is based on 'Facing the real problem for the American Church', *Catholic Herald*, 19 April 2002.

19. 'Attending to the faithful in matters of chastity' was previously published as 'Faith, Gays and Chastity', *Tablet*, 3 March 2007.

20. 'Future trends in Christian ethics in Europe' was given as a talk to a conference bringing together representatives of the Vatican and the Russian Orthodox Church held under the title Christianity, Culture and Moral Values at the Russian Academy of Sciences in Moscow in June 2007.
21. 'Art and vocation' draws upon an article of the same title from *Logos*, summer 2002.
22. 'On religious architecture' draws upon 'On Religious Architecture: A Philosophical Preamble', *Catholic Dossier*, May–June 1997.
23. 'Religious art and religious education' draws upon an article of the same title in *British Journal of Religious Education*, spring 1982.
24. 'On Catholic schools' is based on 'A strong case for state support for Catholic Schools', *Herald*, 25 January 2005.
25. 'Learning and the mind of God' first appeared in *New Blackfriars*, February 1998.

Section I
The Church in the world

1.

Waiting in hope

The contemporary Catholic Church in Britain in the years prior to and following the turn of the millennium has been characterised in a variety of ways: in terms of its social membership, its place in society, its liturgical condition, its participatory decline, and so on. Important as all of these are, they fail to capture what, to speak in psychological terms, might be described as its cognitive and affective state.

In the case of the study of an individual it would certainly be neglectful if, in response to an interest in his or her condition, one spoke only of social standing and general behaviour, and said nothing about states of knowledge and feeling. These may, of course, be difficult matters to determine. For one thing, beliefs and emotions tend to change over time; for another, they do not have well-defined contours. At the level of social group the matter is yet more complex, since states vary and even when they are widespread they cannot simply be aggregated as if the Church as a whole were a single person.

All of this said, it remains possible to speak in general terms, and some reflection on the soul of British Catholicism is necessary if the Church is to know what it needs to do now, particularly in relation to leadership, education and personal formation. It is not enough to reiterate that the proper goal of human life is union with God, for if one is to proceed towards this end one needs to know how far away and in what direction one stands at present, and what the impediments to progress may be.

Whatever I might write is certain to run counter to the experience and state of mind of others, but I report what I have found over several years of speaking in schools, colleges and universities, to lay groups and priests' councils, to 'traditionalists' and 'progressives', to orthodox and heterodox. In addition there is what people say who make approaches in response to talks, pieces of writing and broadcasting. The latter, of course, is a self-selecting sample showing an untypical degree of interest; even so it is a useful source for discerning the state of the Catholic mind in Britain in the opening years of the third millennium.

How then does this appear? The most significant impression, I believe, is the sense of people waiting for things to happen. This has several aspects. There was the expectation, continuing for some while, of the close end of the pontificate of John Paul II, and an associated wonder about what might succeed it.

Catholic criticism of the late Pope ranges from friendly disagreement to barely concealed opposition to both the manner and substance of his papacy. Many found his denegration distasteful but still had hopes which they knew could never be advanced while he remained in office. More generally, however, there was a feeling that the state of things during the period of his decline was an impediment to moving forward, and that while it endured important issues would remain unaddressed, let alone resolved.

All I would add is the observation that as the Pope grew weaker and receded into passivity so his critics grew bolder in expressing their disrespect; and there was increasing uncertainty among more loyal Catholics as to the authoritative status of what emanated from Rome and from other high offices. Petitionary prayers on behalf of the ailing Pope were increasingly apt to be extended to seeking the wellbeing of the papacy and of senior church offices more generally. It is perhaps significant in this connection that George Weigel, biographer and deep admirer of John Paul II, began 2005 (four months before the Pope's death) with a lecture in Washington on the theme 'The Next Pope – And Why He Matters to All of Us'.

Concern also attached to the national hierarchy in consequence of the sexual abuse scandals and the fear that further revelations of abuse or mismanagement might lie ahead. This also takes in the priesthood more generally. It would be too much to say that trust and confidence have given way to suspicion and dread, but there has been a shift in the latter direction to the extent that there is fear of a collapse of priestly life. In times of plenty, a rigorous shaking-out of the seminaries would have been an early move in the process of reform and renewal. Yet the long-term decline in vocations has left bishops struggling to maintain priestly provision and the thought of making admission and training of clergy more demanding seems practically impossible.

That may be a mistake. It is a common feature of admission circumstances that raising the threshold for entry actually increases demand since it elevates the perceived value of the sought-after membership. For that to work, however, there has to be significant demand in the first instance and antecedent valuing of the position. The challenge of increasing good vocations is likely to be most successfully met by raising the standing and the standards of the priesthood, and that needs the co-operation of the laity who in turn need to be remoralised by inspiring leadership.

Meanwhile the situation continues to worsen. Over the last forty years in the UK several dioceses have seen priest numbers drop by more than half, and with an ageing profile the total of serving clergy will have quartered by the end of this decade. Where a large parish might once have been served by several priests it is now typically staffed by one; and increasingly a solitary priest serves several parishes. In some parts of the country the prospect looms of the laity being unable to attend even Sunday Mass without a significant journey to a large centre of population. It is worth bearing in mind, however, that the situation a hundred years ago was also one in which there were very few priests having to serve widely distributed groups of laity. At that point, though, the question was one of material resources and the need was to provide for the spiritual and educational needs of a largely immigrant population. The circumstance today is very different; although there are pockets of material deprivation, on the whole Roman Catholics enjoy the same relatively high standard of living as other Britons. They are no longer a poor people, unable to secure professional employment; or a marginalised group viewing society from its edges. They are, indeed, largely indistinguishable from their neighbours.

That fact may indicate part of the problem. Where Catholics once saw themselves as a persecuted but faithful minority they now value their full membership of society as a whole. So far as this indicates the passing of injustices that is certainly welcome, but they may have gone far beyond finding a place *in* society and become too much a part *of* it. For increasing numbers of cradle Catholics, the Church is now an optional extra; something inessential, more to be sampled on special occasions than to be embraced as the very stuff of life itself. The rest of the time it is either not thought about or else it is viewed as a source of social embarrassment. The religious and moral requirements of the Church are increasing disregarded – if they are even known about.

Whereas the Church was once invoked to judge the world, Catholics increasingly judge it by the standards of the world. The matter has been made worse by the scandals of recent years, for these have increased attacks from without, while sapping the confidence of the laity and diminishing the self-esteem of the clergy. But this is a worsening of something already evident, namely the trend to think that the Church enjoys no special position of authority within one's life; being just another human institution, in part good and in part bad. Against that background it is a wonder that there are any vocations at all.

After all, who would feel a 'vocation' to join a national or international company, particularly when its market image was heavily tarnished?

The truth for believers, however, is that the Church is not (or not merely) a human institution but a divine one, and it is the principal form of Christ's presence in the world. We are Catholics, not as members of a club but as parts of a living body, with each having the responsibility to contribute in some or other way to the wellbeing and development of that body. Vocation is not an option but a vital imperative. Just as a blood cell or an organ must function if it is to survive and the body is to flourish, so the Catholic must serve if he or she is not to die in spirit, and the Church in the world is not to be diminished.

With this in mind priests and parents should be insistent, not hesitant, in pressing the universal call to service in the life of the Church. The phrase 'everyone has a vocation' can be said and heard as a morale-boosting banality, but it can also be preached as statement of responsibility. Every Catholic has a duty to contribute to the Church through active service. That service may be as a Catholic parent, as a Catholic teacher, as a Catholic academic, as a Catholic carer, as a Catholic lawyer, as a Catholic priest, as a Catholic religious, and so on.

The truth I am aiming at lies between on the one hand, the claim that everyone must practice as an announcedly Catholic such and such, a Catholic teacher, say; and on the other the idea that it is enough to be a teacher *and* a Catholic. In between lies a subtler combination: that of letting one's Catholicism inform one's practice and of letting one's practice be witness to one's Catholicism. The question to pose in every church, school, and home is that of what each person's Catholic vocation will be: will it be as a (Catholic) parent, or as a (Catholic) teacher, or as a (Catholic) religious, or whatever. Vocation is not an option, it is a responsibility, and it should be preached unmistakably and repeatedly as such: your Church and your God need you, how (exactly) do you plan to serve them?

The task of raising the standing and the standards of the priesthood is not impossible but it will take determined and sustained efforts on all sides. As it is, however, the trend to bureaucratise the clergy, subjecting them to ever-more administrative demands, and quasi-clericising the laity, demoralises the former and confuses the latter. It should be the aim of diocesan offices to relieve priests of paperwork, and of bishops to make clear that the role of the laity is not to substitute for priestly functions (principally celebrating the sacraments, though also related adult sacramental preparation and spiritual direction) but to be active in parochial activities and the lay apostolate.

Feelings of uncertainty and some confusion about the religious leadership of the Church are paralleled on the cognitive side by doubts about the rational credentials of the faith. Some readers will recall past presentations of Catholicism in which their personal piety was inspired and deepened by sacramental liturgies that combined aesthetic forms and a rich theology. Alongside this lay belief in a supernatural order revealed in apparitions, saintly intercessions, miraculous cures, and other mystical manifestations.

One could see these different elements as corresponding to two kinds of cognitive need. The first being for a rational foundation for belief, often provided for by versions of traditional arguments for the existence and goodness of God. The second being for direct empirical evidence of God and his works, answered by experiences of a world beyond nature.

No doubt these latter ways of believing involved credulity and superstition; certainly popular presentations of arguments for the existence and goodness of God could be fallacious. Yet Catholic faith will not long survive where mystical sensibility and philosophical theology are purged or even just neglected. St Augustine writes in the *Confessions* of how God made us for Himself and how our hearts are restless until they find Him. If that is true, and Catholics can hardly doubt it, then it is to be expected that there are cognitive and affective ways and means of recognising God's existence. That behoves us to be open to the idea that reason and experience may both provide warrant for belief.

Until quite recently this was not just assented to but pursued through writings about Catholic mystics, artists, philosophers and theologians. But for all that there are a number who continue to celebrate and explore the Catholic cultural tradition, the main areas of interest now seem to be ethical, social and political. These are certainly important and relevant fields, yet often Catholic contributions seem mere echoes of notions already familiar from the secular world.

Just as there is a feeling of uncertainty in relation to the future of the institutional Church, so there is a sense of awaiting a renewal of Catholic apologetics and cultural creativity. In neither case is the mood of expectation accompanied by optimism; but neither, save among the disaffected traditionalist and progressive fringes, is it marked by despair. From the point of view of the Catholic understanding of Providence that is probably the right demeanour, since the proper response to doubt about the present is not human optimism but religious hope. It is in that spirit that the faithful are waiting and praying for relief in times of trouble.

2.

A Church and its critics

For reasons that are not altogether easy to fathom, but about which I shall speculate, secular society now seems particularly keen on criticising the policies and personalities of Roman Catholicism, most especially its popes.

Catholic education and church schools have come under renewed attack as maintaining, if not initiating, sectarian division. In the wake of contrasting responses to John Cornwell's book *Hitler's Pope: The Secret History of Pius XII* (1999) heated exchanges continue over the character of Pius XII and of the papacy in general. A further issue arising in Scotland, but which almost certainly has counterparts elsewhere, was of the Catholic Church's financial support for a pregnant twelve-year-old whose parents had applied for help under the late Cardinal Winning's Pro-Life Initiative. I want to explore what may be the deep sources of such anti-Catholic criticism by considering these three issues in turn.

Formal education is a practice in need of a justification. In Scotland since the fifteenth century and in England and Wales since the nineteenth, laws have been passed requiring parents to attend to the education of their children. Although this can be done at home, in practice such laws amount to compulsory schooling. So familiar is this that we rarely consider let alone challenge its rationale, but social compulsion backed by legal sanction stands in need of a supporting argument.

There are two broad forms of justification for it: the first looks to the interests of the child, the second to the well-being of society. In each case the justifications divide between one's focusing on the intrinsic value of being educated, and one's looking to the consequential benefits of knowledge. In the 1960s and 70s, for example, there was much talk of the role of schooling being to realise the unique potential of the individual child. In reaction to this, and in response to economic imperatives introduced by Margaret Thatcher and maintained by Tony Blair, the 1980s and 90s were dominated by emphasis on the need of schools to serve society by equipping it with an enterprising Information Technology (IT)-trained workforce.

Shallow and partial as they may be, these contrasting rationales are, in effect, 'philosophies of education' – though it is perhaps significant that in the last two decades this branch of educational theory has struggled to survive in the UK. Catholicism, by contrast, has always been and remains deeply committed to the importance of educational practice being rooted in a philosophy of human nature and of society. Some of the earliest Christian writings concern education and virtually every major Catholic theologian has addressed the issue. In the thirteenth century St Thomas Aquinas explored the nature of teaching and learning in his *De Veritate*, and in the nineteenth Cardinal Newman wrote *On the Idea of a University*, the first and still the best rationale of higher education, and probably the best defence of Catholic educational theories in any language.

What links the centuries of Catholic thinking about education is a unifying belief in the special character of human beings. Each is, according to Catholic faith, *imago dei*: an image of God: a thinking, acting being fitted for eternal life in company with others and with its Creator. At the same time, however, there is the mystery of original sin – not, as some Protestant renderings, a state of total depravity but an inherent liability to twist and turn away from the good. Like the growth of a plant human development is trainable and correctable, but unlike a plant human formation involves guiding the interior life as well as the exterior form.

So emerges the Catholic philosophy of education. Earthly life is a preparation for eternity and the interior quality and general orientation of that life depend very largely on social and cultural influences, most especially on home and school. Whatever ethnic or tribal associations may (or may not) gather around these institutions – and the tendency for that to happen has nothing at all to do with whether or not they are religious – it is both natural and proper that those of the Catholic faith (as of other distinctive denominations and faiths) should put religion at the heart of education. Those best believe what they teach who teach what they believe, and who do so in the interests of children and inspired by an ennobling vision of what it is to be human.

It was just such a vision that inspired John Henry Newman to convert to Catholicism in 1845 and led him to deliver in Dublin in 1852 his lectures on the idea of a university. In between times two Oratories had been established, in Old Oscott and in London out of the second of which, in 1863, was founded the Oratory School to which the Blairs chose to send their sons – a school whose primary aim is spiritual formation and not preparation for the employment market.

What has secular society to offer Catholics and other Christians in place of church schools? No unifying vision; no deep cultural perspective; no distinctive personal and social values; no ennobling conception of the human condition. It unsurprising that a culture increasingly given to materialism, hedonism and egotism, and visibly adrift on the seas of relativism, should increase the frequency and intensity of its attacks on the Catholic school system. For the latter is the principal means by which the most ancient Western philosophical and theological system is transmitted to the next generation. Interestingly, in recent times the Archbishop of Canterbury has argued that Britain needs more church schools because 'they stand for values which parents perceive to belong to our heritage as a nation and the ethical standards and moral norms that go back to the teaching of Christ'. The case for the preservation of Catholic schools is ultimately, I believe, the case for the preservation of Christianity.

Turning to the furore surrounding the publication of John Cornwell's *Hitler's Pope* the most significant feature of this, I think, was the fact that its appearance served as a lightning conductor of anti-Catholic sentiment. For the most part the opinions expressed did not depend on a reading of the book itself; and even when it had been read reviewers hostile to Catholicism went far beyond their brief.

By way of a case study I consider the reviews by Frank McGlynn in the *Herald* and in the *Independent*. Both were marked – and I would say marred – by evident personal animus and gratuitous attacks upon the then Pope. The axe grinding is deafening in the opening sentence of his *Herald* review: 'John Paul II has often made plain his contempt for the modern world and his arrogant assumption that he is infallible not just in faith and morals, but in politics, ethics, and even cosmology.' So far as balanced critical assessment is concerned readers are assured that 'No praise is too high for this book.'

For my own part I am not able to judge the quality or originality of Cornwell's research. His earlier books include investigative reporting of other controversial Catholic subjects. *A Thief in the Night* (1989) concerns the death of John Paul I and *Powers of Darkness, Powers of Light* (1991) is an exploration of purportedly miraculous and supernatural phenomena. Though once a seminarian Cornwell lost his vocation and his faith in his twenties, and his attitude to Catholicism as reported in these and later books such as *Breaking Faith: The Pope, The People and the Fate of Catholicism* (2001) and *The Pope in Winter: The Dark Face of John Paul II's Papacy* (2004) is an ambiguous one.

I mention that fact because a number of reviewers

enthusiastic about Cornwell's anti-Pius conclusions quote with approval from the preface to *Hitler's Pope* in which he writes of the attitudes of 'Catholics of his generation' and expresses the view that his investigations were begun in the expectation of clearing Pius of the charges. The suggestion seized upon by reviewers is of a devout Catholic shaken by his discoveries, as if that *pro hominem* consideration lends his case greater credibility.

So far as the substance of Cornwell's accusations is concerned it is worth comparing McGlynn's unqualified endorsement with the measured assessment of the Anglican church historian Sir Owen Chadwick. Chadwick describes the book as 'a serious study of a very complex character tossed about in the most tragic series of crises ever to afflict Europe' and notes Cornwell's inclination to exaggerate what Pius had the power to do and to criticise him for things for which he was not in fact responsible. McGlynn, by contrast, has nothing but bad to say of Pius (as of John Paul II) and writes of Cornwell's 'labours reveal[ing] an extremely dark figure of the far right'.

The clear fact is that *Hitler's Pope* was a 'God send' to those predisposed to think ill of the papacy; in other words to those in the grip of an anti-Catholic prejudice. The office of pope is now routinely denounced as an authoritarian institution and its occupants derided as arrogant and tyrannical. It is a deep irony that while John Paul II was characterised as an oppressive figure by Western secularists he was celebrated in the former Soviet Bloc as one of the principal agents in the collapse of totalitarianism, and in the Third World as an advocate of the poor against the forces of international capitalism. These facts barely register with critics whose opinions are formed out of antecedent hostility to the theological, philosophical and moral principles of Catholicism.

Such hostility has also been evident in denunciations of the Pro-Life Initiative's support of the pregnant twelve-year-old. Launched in 1997 this initiative was an attempt to back moral principle with practical means. One might have thought, therefore, that it would be welcome as an appropriate response to the criticism that an anti-abortion stance is a luxury that those in need cannot afford. However the policy has been criticised since it began, and the particular case of the twelve-year-old brought forth ever-sharper denunciation. The campaign manager of the Abortion Law Reform Society was quoted as saying: 'I am appalled to learn what the Church is doing. I would say Cardinal Winning has allowed his religious principles to totally override his common sense.'

One might conclude from this and the other criticisms that the Catholic Church and the philosophy it embodies are in deep trouble: sectarian, illiberal, arrogant, and uncaring, it is a world-view whose day is done. My own judgement is that the very contrary is the case. It is not Catholicism that is in crisis but secular society, and these various attacks provide some evidence for this. Catholicism is criticised for being too narrow in failing to take account of developments in society, and for being too broad in its ambition to encompass all human life in a single philosophy. It is accused of failing to use its authority to denounce evil, and condemned for presuming that it has any authority to do so. It is charged with making a fetish of suffering and death, and of making another fetish out of promoting and protecting life.

There is surely something odd in all of this. Could it be that the world has gone astray, that Catholicism has held fast to fundamental truths, and that it is now reviled for its steadfastness? What the healthy judges to be right, the fevered and the chilled find to be too hot or too cold. Philosophers make a point of distinguishing contraries from contradictories: in the case of the latter one must be true, in the case of the former both may be false. A meal may be neither too large nor too small, too hot nor too cold but only seem so to those of abnormal appetites and sensitivities. Similarly it could be that denunciations of Catholic teachings reveal something similar about the distorted viewpoints of the critics.

Underlying the Catholic belief in the importance of religious education, the necessity of teaching authorities, the inviolability of life, the sanctity of the family and so on, is a view of the human condition that sees us as basically good, but at risk from threats and dangers some of which arise, tragically, within us. Tempted by the ideal of natural perfectibility we endeavour to eliminate frailty and vulnerability and become ever more extreme in our efforts. Pornography sets aside the vulnerability of love in favour of momentary and local satisfaction. Abortion and euthanasia set aside the reality of pain and inconvenience in the name of 'practical common-sense solutions'. Genetic technologies are pursued in the hope of being able to create multiple embryos from which to choose the best and destroy the rest.

Some of the same papers that reported the criticisms of the Pro-Life Initiative contained an insert inviting readers to 'mark the millennium' by buying a limited edition doll's carriage. For just £500, each of 5,000 purchasers could gave acquired a craftsman-made model pram. Nostalgic imagery of little girls and dolls accompanied the reality of a babyless carriage. Real human beings are being aborted for reasons of convenience, while time, talent and money are consumed adorning houses with childless toys.

In the same week reports of clashes between UN and Indonesian forces were accompanied by a picture of an East Timorese refugee kissing a vandalised statue of the Virgin Mary inside the burned-out home of Bishop Carlos Belo. This is the sort of peasant piety that is grist to the mill of anti-Catholic critics, but it is of a piece with belief in an order of goodness and justice by which human wrong doing can be judged. What authority can the cultural relativists and advocates of moral subjectivism invoke that in any way equals that of Bishop Belo in condemning tyranny and despotism? And who is listening if they should feign to possess it?

Not only are basic Catholic ethical positions defensible, they are gaining allies among former critics. In the United

States and to some extent in Britain there is an emerging appreciation of Catholic moral opposition to sterilisation, abortion, euthanasia, pornography and promiscuity. Many feminists and other radicals have moved to a more 'conservative' position on sexuality, and there is a growing Gays and Lesbians for Life movement. At the same time there is increasingly widespread doubt about the moral resources and general health of secular society.

I view these matters as a Catholic and as a philosopher, and I make no pretence to be a neutral commentator. But my religious and intellectual positions are mutually supportive, and in a time of social crisis neutrality is a stance that we cannot afford and for which our children will not thank us. It is strange to criticise a religious leader such as the late Cardinal Winning for allowing his religious principles to override his common sense. It is yet more dangerous to proceed in the name of common sense without recourse to principles. That way lie crude pragmatism and a deeper crisis.

By way of conclusion, it is worth considering again the contrasting verdicts of the journalist McGlynn and the historian Chadwick and comparing them with the considered judgement of John Cornwell himself five years after the publication of *Hitler's Pope*. Writing in the *Economist* (9 December 2004) he concluded

> I would now argue, in the light of the debates and evidence following *Hitler's Pope*, that Pius XII had so little scope of action that it is impossible to judge the motives for his silence during the war, while Rome was under the heel of Mussolini and later occupied by Germany.

For reasons too obvious to identify this opinion was not widely reported.

3.

Catholicism in an age of liberalism

It is common for orthodox Catholics to bemoan the effects
of Western secularisation and to attribute many of these to
the influence of liberal thought: rising incidences of ille-
gitimacy, widespread availability and practice of abortion,
increasing divorce rates, eroticism in the media and ever-
more explicit pornography. All of these and many more
problems and vices are laid at the door of 'liberalism'.
From this point of view any relaxation of social restraints
is an invitation to disregard propriety and the moral law.
Thus liberalism is regarded as the philosophy of license, or
as a charter for vice.

Since Western Europe and North America seem
committed to liberal principles it is worth asking whether
liberalism is in fact as black as this Catholic view paints it.
I ask this notwithstanding that I once authored an essay
entitled 'Can a Catholic be a Liberal?' and answered with a
qualified 'no'. The point is largely definitional, though far
from trivially so. When moral conservatives speak of
'liberalism' they more often have in mind a set of permissive attitudes than a fundamental political principal; yet it
is at the level of philosophical principles that the case for
or against liberalism needs to be decided.

This said, there are connections between the holding of
political principles and the advancement of moral attitudes. Thus those who think there is nothing morally
wrong about abortion are likely to favour permissive legislation; by the same token it is difficult – psychologically –

to maintain the view that the state has no right, let alone any duty, to prevent abortions, while also believing that to kill a foetus is as grave a human injustice as can be performed. Yet it is important to consider whether the tension may be psychological rather than logical. For there is one version of political liberalism – *neutralist liberalism* – which maintains, without apparent contradiction, that it is not legitimate to allow moral considerations to shape the laws and institutions of the state.

Such a position is narrowly political, concerning civil and criminal legislation and sanction. Thus it is not within its scope to pronounce upon the moral character of actions and policies. Relatedly, neutralist liberalism tends to draw a sharp distinction between the private domain and the public sphere and locate morality in the former and politics in the latter. These distinctions in place it then seems possible to say 'I am wholly opposed to abortion as a matter of private morality but I think it should be allowed as a matter of public political policy.' The governing ideal behind this view is the moral neutrality of the state; the thesis that it is no business of political society to advance or protect any particular conception of the good – be it that of Christian moral theology, atheistic humanism or 'gay culture'.

There is something elegantly simple about this idea yet it is untenable – and not just because the real world is complex. The point against the neutral state is not that it is impractical but that it is ultimately confused. The public and the private, the moral and the political are convenient classifications but they do not mark wholly separate spheres. In one sense of 'private' it may be nobody else's business what one does in the privacy of one's own home, but in another sense the fact that an action is performed 'in private' has nothing to do with whether or not it is a matter of legitimate public and political concern.

The truth of the matter is that morality does and should constrain the public sphere; the private may be immoral, and the immorality may be of sorts that the state has a

duty to inhibit. So says Catholic social teaching, and so
says everyone else who thinks it is not a matter of political
indifference whether, for example, children are sexually
abused in the privacy of their parents' homes. So the idea
of the morally disinterested state has to be qualified, but
once this is conceded the neutralist liberal has lost the
argument. It is then a matter for discussion how morally
committed the state should be, at which point the opponents of abortion, pornography and whatever else may
make their case. Not only must Catholics be opposed to
neutralist liberalism; no one who thinks there are moral
rights and wrongs that are of concern to society can maintain a philosophy of political indifference.

This might seem a fitting point on which to end, but I
need to extend the discussion a little further because
secular political theorists have themselves come to see the
inadequacies of the neutralist form of liberalism and are
now trying to give other accounts of what liberty in political society should amount to. Indeed it is becoming
common to speak of the rise of a new kind of 'perfectionist' liberalism. This way of speaking, however, is doubly
misleading: the view in question is neither new nor liter-
ally perfectionist. Its guiding thought is to be found in
such nineteenth-century writers as Mill and de
Tocqueville and it is less concerned with perfection than
with improvement.

The idea is that society should be ordered in such a way
as befits rational beings who live together as citizens and
who need to be able to develop physically, psychologically,
socially and morally if they are to attain value in their
lives. On this account, therefore, liberty may be politically
constrained by moral requirements; but freedom is also a
value to be protected and promoted by the state because it
is only through free choice that agents may become
morally good. The state cannot make us free but it may not
deny us our freedom save when to exercise it would be
intolerably immoral.

How immoral is that? It is not for abstract political

theory to say. We need to look at the moral values in particular societies, and at the religious and philosophical sources of these values in order to determine their significance. In other words we need to engage in moral enquiry. Recognising that this, morally engaged, form of liberalism need not be at odds with religious claims *per se*, the Christian has cause to take it seriously, and perhaps even to adopt it as best expressing recent social teaching. As John Paul II observed:

> There is need to recover the *basic elements of a vision of the relationship between civil law and moral law*, which are put forward by the Church, but which are also part of the patrimony of the great juridical traditions of humanity ... The real purpose of civil law is to guarantee an ordered social coexistence in true justice. (*Evangelium Vitae* §71)

Believers should thus feel more optimistic about the position of Christianity at what may be the dawning of a new age of liberalism.

The Western world may be turning back towards the idea of a morally committed social order. Certainly, given signs of movement in that direction, Catholics should be doing everything they can to encourage such a return: embracing an ideal of freedom under law subject to morality. But while a more noble and morally responsive notion of individual freedom is a necessary corrective to some of the damaging trends of recent years, by itself it fails to engage what may be the more profound malaise of Western society.

Following the Second World War there was a great deal of questioning in philosophical, theological and literary circles about the meaning of human life and the future of Western civilisation. This questioning was greatest in countries most deeply affected by the hostilities and among those who had once again been the subject of systematic persecution – the Jews. In the case of the latter the question was posed, 'Where was the God of Abraham and Isaac when his people were gassed and burned in the death camps?' But Christians also found it hard to contemplate such pervasive and unrelieved evil. What had become of the efficacy of petitionary prayer and the loving providence of God? Secular intellectuals were hardly better placed to comprehend the scale of events. The humanist renaissance, the age of enlightenment, the rise of democratic politics and the development of mass education had suggested a process of intellectual and social improvement. Yet the evils embodied in Nazism and the relentless violence shown on all sides seemed evidence of a potential for depravity that was difficult to explain in purely natural terms.

As the years passed and generations grew up who had no memory of the war and no experience of mass unemployment and poverty, attention shifted from the problems of evil to the fashioning of a new culture: popular, participatory, light, bright and liberating. In the 1980s a new economic order developed in which labour-intensive manufacturing came to be replaced by technology-based industry and service employment. Gone the grit and smoke, the men-only bars and the women-only bingo halls, to be replaced by brightly lit industrial units, shopping centres, theme bars with guest ales and chilled white wine on tap, and then – and increasingly – home-based, electronic entertainment.

Now the killing and mutilation are back. In Central Europe, as well as in Africa and Asia, we have seen the bodies pile up. On screen, mutant warriors, street gangs and vigilantes blast away at one another's bodies. And increasingly sex is blended in with the violence. Videos and video games permit millions to indulge tastes that hitherto were largely restricted to the wealthy few. And this powerful cocktail is not sipped at, but consumed regularly and in large quantities. There is real killing too: abortion, domestic murder, and creeping euthanasia.

The post-war questions re-assert themselves. What underlies our capacity for good and evil? How can the baser elements be trained or contained? What can we teach with authority and hand on with confidence to future generations? Catholics should be better placed than their non-religious neighbours and workmates to address these questions, and they should be less prey to some of the problems I have mentioned. My sense, however, is that as things stand we are more part of the problem than part of the solution. Aside from the very elderly who retain a sense of the order of grace, Catholics seem to be as hedonistic and materialist as any others – and this makes us worse, for we are supposed to the yeast that leavens the dough!

What has gone wrong and how can it be rectified? Catholic traditionalists will complain of an over-accommodation to the values of the late twentieth century and urge the need of liturgical restoration and the necessity of the older doctrinal instruction. Liberals will argue that there has been insufficient acknowledgement of the modern and post-modern worlds, and press the need to promote justice and peace outside the Church, and to effect reforms within it in concerning the priesthood and the teachings on sex and marriage.

Significant as these issues may be, to focus on them would be to distract ourselves from a much more important matter, one that undercuts the division between traditionalists and progressives and one which will determine the future of Catholicism and the value of its contribution to Western civilisation in the coming millennium – that is the development of spirituality and the recovery of the sense of the supernatural. Contemporary Catholicism is almost exclusively concerned with externals, with liturgical forms, with social action, with ethical conduct, and so on. Without questioning the importance of these I would suggest that there is an urgent need to turn inwards and to reflect on the condition of the individual soul and on the interior life of the Church itself.

The classic authors of French Catholic spirituality such as Francis de Sales, Brother Lawrence of the Resurrection, and Jeanne-Pierre de Caussade: each lived in times of great unsettlement and decadence, in many respects quite like our own. Each found ways of nurturing the interior life of those whom they directed, cultivating in them a sense of the continuous presence of God and of the fact that human beings live in two dimensions: that of the natural world, and that of the supernatural order.

Those who came to understand this changed their values and devoted themselves to improving the lives of others. De Caussade wrote of the 'sure and solid foundation' of Christian life being 'to give ourselves to God and to put ourselves entirely in his hands, body and soul'. This 'abandonment' both flows from and deepens the common experience of human falleness. But it is not quietism. For those who partake in what de Caussade termed 'the sacrament of the present moment' the necessity of active service to God and others is vividly clear. It is evident that we are on a slope and sliding; standing still is not an option. We must recover the true Catholic insight that 'action follows upon being', in other words that things act according to their nature, and recover the practice of spiritual formation by which to improve our natures and thus our actions.

4.

Taking faith seriously

In May 2007 on the occasion for the annual Day for Life, and in anticipation of the fortieth anniversary of the passing of the UK Abortion Act, Cardinal O'Brien preached in St Mary's Cathedral in Edinburgh on the subject of abortion. In the course of his sermon he spoke of the seven million pregnancies terminated in the UK since 1967 describing this as 'an unspeakable crime' and a 'wanton killing of innocents'. By way of indicating its daily scale he observed the following:

> We're told by statisticians that the equivalent of a class-room of children every day are being aborted in their mothers' womb – basically murdered in their mothers' womb ... We are killing – in our country – the equivalent of a classroom of kids every single day. Can you imagine that? Two Dunblane massacres a day in our country going on and on. And when's it going to stop?

These remarks were described by some as insensitive and inflammatory; but what attracted greatest attention and criticism was his call to Catholic politicians to consider their position with regard to supporting abortion legislation. He said:

> I ask them [Catholic politicians] to examine their consciences and discern if they are playing any part in sustaining this social evil. I remind them to avoid co-oper-

ating in the unspeakable crime of abortion and the barrier
such co-operation erects to receiving Holy Communion.

I want to place these reactions to the Cardinal's intervention within a broader context of increasing opposition to
Catholic teachings, but before doing so to examine central
aspects of the abortion debate. Here it is also relevant to
recall events from the far side of the Atlantic. On 5 November 2003 President George W. Bush signed into law the
Partial-Birth Abortion Act and in April 2004 did the same
for the Unborn Victims of Violence Act. These acts were
perceived to favour the pro-life cause: for the first bans a
form of late term abortion, while the second recognises a
'child in utero' as a legal victim. In the following months,
as the November presidential election approached, the
Democratic candidate Senator John Kerry came under
pressure over his contrasting support for liberal abortion
laws.

To his credit Kerry made no secret of his commitments.
He had consistently voted in favour of pro-choice abortion
legislation, and had co-sponsored a Senate amendment to
the Partial-Birth Abortion Bill, affirming that the 1973 Roe
vs Wade Supreme Court judgment recognising abortion as
a constitutional right was correctly decided. He then
announced that if elected President he would nominate
only pro-choice judges to the Federal Supreme Court. This
last was a commitment of considerable political significance, given that the Court has the power to determine the
legality of both federal and state actions.

Given this background of controversy and debate it may
be helpful to offer a philosophical perspective on these
issues. In particular, I want to focus on the ethics and the
politics of abortion. First, then, the moral argument
against termination, which in its simplest form runs as
follows:

1. it is always and everywhere wrong intentionally to kill
   an innocent human being;

2. an embryo or foetus in the womb is an innocent human being;
3. therefore, it is always and everywhere wrong intentionally to kill an embryo or foetus in the womb.

Certainly there are those who will deny that it is always wrong intentionally to kill the innocent. Utilitarianism and other theories aptly termed 'consequentialist' maintain that the moral value of any action is determined by the overall good it produces, and since in some circumstances more good may result from intentionally killing an innocent person than from refraining from doing so, in such a case the killing is not merely permitted but required. Many readers are likely to agree that this implication is sufficient reason to reject consequentialist ethics. Even so, one may nonetheless reject the anti-abortion conclusion by arguing that an embryo or foetus is not a human being. This connects with the issue of whether modern Catholic teaching about the origins of life is at odds with what was taught in the past, and whether it is refuted by contemporary embryology.

Critics are apt to point out that Aquinas maintained that human 'ensoulment' only occurs a month or so after conception for males, and at three months for females. This differentiation ought, however, to alert us to the possibility of his having a false embryology; and indeed it is so. The details are complex but in brief it follows from Aquinas's account of human beings that the human soul or organising principle only comes into existence when the body generated by the parents is sufficiently organised to be disposed for it. This principle requires the material organisation sufficient for *the development of* those organs that support all of the operations proper to the human species.

On the basis of mistaken embryological assumptions, Aquinas himself believed that such organisation did not occur until the distinct organs were visibly present, but when his principle is applied to what is now known about

reproduction-gestation the conclusion is that the organisation of the body required for human ensoulment occurs
at or close to conception; for even at the two-cell stage the
cells of the developing organism are differentiated,
serving as primordia of different systems of organs. The
fact of monozygotic twinning, in which a single zygote
splits to produce two embryos, has been taken to imply
that the original product of conception is not a human
individual and that the latter only comes to exist after a
couple of weeks. But all that such twinning shows is that at
the earliest stage of embryonic development the degree of
specialisation of the cells is limited so that groups of them
may, if divided, become whole organisms. It does not
follow that prior to division the embryo is a mere mass of
cells and not a unitary human organism.

Not only are scholars generally aware of the scientific
flaws in Aquinas's views about human ensoulment, but the
Catholic Church itself has made reference to them in its
declarations. In the important 1974 'Declaration on
Procured Abortion', the Sacred Congregation for the
Doctrine of the Faith states that

> In the course of history, the Fathers of the Church, her
> Pastors and her Doctors have taught the same doctrine
> [that human life must be protected and favored from the
> beginning, just as at the various stages of its develop-
> ment]—the various opinions on the infusion of the spiri-
> tual soul did not introduce any doubt about the illicitness
> of abortion. It is true that in the Middle Ages, when the
> opinion was generally held that the spiritual soul was not
> present until after the first few weeks ... But it was never
> denied at that time that procured abortion, even during the
> first days, was an objectively grave fault.

The principal factor in effecting a change in the Church's
teaching about the nature of early abortion was the development of a modern understanding of the ovum, the
process of fertilisation and the principle of foetal self-
development. Allowing that there may be some indetermi-

nacy in best current accounts of when exactly a new human being begins to exist, the Church nevertheless teaches that this should be deemed to occur at conception. The point is stated clearly in *Donum Vitae*

> Thus the fruit of human generation, from the first moment of its existence, that is to say from the moment the zygote has formed, demands the unconditional respect that is morally due to the human being in his bodily and spiritual totality.

So much for the fundamental ethics of abortion: what of its immediate politics? The US is the country in which the issue of morality and law are now most sharply focused. President Bush long declared himself to be pro-life and to that end signed into law the two measures referred to above. Senator Kerry also declared himself 'pro-life' but opposed the Partial-Birth Abortion Bill, stating that 'This is a dangerous effort to undermine a woman's right to choose, which is a constitutional amendment I will always fight to protect.'

Unsurprisingly perhaps, Senator Kerry had quoted to him the document *The Participation of Catholics in Political Life* produced by the Sacred Congregation for the Doctrine of the Faith, which states that: 'A well-formed Christian conscience does not permit one to vote for a political programme or an individual law which contradicts the fundamental contents of faith and morals.'

Kerry replied as follows:- 'It is not appropriate in the US for a legislator to legislate personal religious beliefs for the rest of the country,' and others of like-mind are apt to speak of a 'constitutional separation of Church and State', objecting to the idea that church officials might command politicians to legislate in accord with church teachings. But these gestures only serve to display a fistful of red herrings.

First, there is no unambiguous constitutional separation of religion and politics. The first amendment to the US Constitution states that 'Congress shall pass no law respecting an establishment of religion, or prohibiting the free exercise thereof.' This prevents the federal government from sponsoring, supporting, or actively involving itself with a particular religion, but it does not debar members of Congress from informing their consciences from religious sources.

Second, whether it may be improper or imprudent for clerics to instruct their fellow believers in political matters is a different question from whether believers involved in politics should allow religious ideas to inform their thinking.

Third, the anti-abortion argument that I gave, and which is invoked in relevant church documents, makes no appeal to religious revelation.

Fourth, the refrain recited by Senator Kerry 'Personally I disagree with abortion, but in a free society women must have the right to choose' obscures an important distinction between endorsement and toleration. It is one thing, having lost the policy debate, to tolerate permissive abortion laws, and quite another to propose that there should be permissive legislation and to vote for it. Advocacy of the latter on the part of those who claim to be anti-abortion indicates confusion or indifference.

Until recently I would have said that to their credit, and notwithstanding notable exceptions, these are faults to which British legislators (in all political parties) have been less liable, but reaction to Cardinal O'Brien's sermon gives reason to wonder whether the situation may be changing.

Abortion is a serious moral and political issue, but unlike many others confronting us it is not one that is remote from the experience or influence of most individuals. Perhaps too often, and too easily, Catholics seek to align themselves with causes proclaimed by the world; for it is an important test of who we are, and of where we stand, whether we are willing to oppose ourselves to the temper of the times. There is no virtue in approving what is approved of, nor any defence in having only followed the order of the day.

Anyone who claims to be shocked by the Catholic view that intentional abortion is objectively a case of murderous killing is either ignorant of the Church's long-held view or else feigning surprise in an effort to cast that judgement as beyond belief. Of course, the view is open to objection, as are other Catholic moral teachings about marriage, capital punishment and the justice of war, but it is surprising to see them being reported as if newly discovered. They have long been proclaimed and argued for in detail and at length.

If their extent and specificity, and the conviction with which they are declared seem unusual, and out of keeping with the style of other sources of public interventions, this may be due to the pervasive influence of relativism according to which there is no such thing as objective moral truth, let alone an overall system of truths. To the extent that the relativist can or wishes to make sense of moral seriousness it amounts not to a determination to discover universal values and requirements, but rather to a resolve to make authentic personal choices: 'doing what you feel is right'.

This trend from objective truth to subjective conviction has taken its toll on other comprehensive world-views besides Catholicism. Time was when those interested in justice debated the claims of egalitarian socialism and liberal capitalism, and those concerned with history discussed whether it was inevitable, rationally intelligible, or merely one thing after another. Likewise others debated whether human beings were naturally good or depraved, whether existence was meaningful or absurd, and whether there could be any hope of personal happiness apart from social or religious salvation.

These contrasts and oppositions, and the arguments on either side, would once have been familiar to educated readers but increasingly value and meaning are terms of market assessment and lifestyle choice. The very idea that one's happiness might depend upon answering fundamental existential questions, and that there are comprehensive philosophical and theological systems addressed to resolving these seems to have been lost sight of, or perhaps rejected.

One does not have to go far to find reminders of how, not so long ago, it was otherwise, and of how Catholicism was understood by educated people even when it was denied by them. In his book *The Unknown God: Agnostic Essays* (2004), the former priest and ex-Master of Balliol College, Oxford, Sir Anthony Kenny discusses the attitudes of several nineteenth- and twentieth-century 'greats' to the question of religion, which often took the form of choosing, and sometimes oscillating between atheism, agnosticism and Catholicism. At one point he quotes Sir Leslie Stephens, author, mountaineer and father of Virginia Woolf, writing of John Henry Newman (a figure to whom Kenny returns often). Stephens writes:

> He declares, as innumerable writers of lesser power have declared, that there is no medium, in true philosophy, between Atheism and Catholicity, and that a perfectly consistent mind, under those circumstances in which it finds itself here below, must embrace either the one or the other.

That was at the end of the nineteenth century and one might view it as a curiosity of the age. But consider the following from a hero of twentieth-century liberal thought. Writing in 1942 in a review of the first three of T. S. Elliot's *Four Quartets* George Orwell remarks

> Sooner or later one is obliged to adopt a positive stance towards life and society. It would be putting it to crudely to say that every poet in our time must either die young, enter the Catholic Church, or join the Communist Party, but in fact the escape from the consciousness of futility is along these lines.

To contemporary secular liberals this may seem almost as shocking as Cardinal O'Brien's sermon. Certainly they would be discomforted by Orwell's hostility to the idea of abortion as expressed through the main character of *Keep the Aspidistra Flying*:

> For the first time he grasped, with the only kind of knowledge that matters, what they were really talking about. The words 'a baby' took on a new significance. They did not mean any longer a mere abstract disaster, they meant a bud of flesh, a bit of himself, down there in her belly, alive and growing ... He knew then that it was a dreadful thing they were contemplating – a blasphemy, if that word had any meaning. Yet if it had been put otherwise he might not have recoiled from it. ... 'No fear!' he said. 'Whatever happens we're not going to do that. It's disgusting.'

Elsewhere Orwell wrote of how 'very few people, a part from Catholics themselves, seem to have grasped that the Church is to be taken seriously'. Orwell understood its commitment to 'infinite truth' and respected it for that, though he himself rejected religion. Others of his generation, however, like others before and since saw the depth of its teachings and entered the Church.

The converts of the twentieth-century number, among creative artists and writers, R. H. Benson, Sir Lennox Berkeley, G. K. Chesterton, Christopher Dawson, David Jones, Graham Greene, Sir Alec Guinness, Ronald Knox, Sir Compton McKenzie, Marshall McLuhan, Malcolm Muggeridge, Alfred Noyes, Siegfried Sassoon, Edith Sitwell, Muriel Spark, Graham Sutherland, J. R. R. Tolkien, and Evelyn Waugh. Since this might be thought to reflect the appeal of fantasy to the imaginative mind it is worth adding a list of leading contemporary British and American philosophers who also converted to Roman Catholicism: Elizabeth Anscombe, Frederick Copleston, Sir Michael Dummett, Peter Geach, Alasdair MacIntyre, Nicholas Rescher, and Bas van Fraassen (joining such Continental philosopher converts as René Girard, Gabriel Marcel, Jacques Maritain, Max Scheler, and Edith Stein).

Before reaching for some further explanation of why it is that serious thinkers might have been drawn to Catholi-

cism it may be worth considering the possibility that as
Orwell saw 'it is to be taken seriously'. G. K. Chesterton
once described philosophy as 'thought that has been
thought out', adding that 'man has no alternative except
being influenced by thought that has been thought out and
influenced by thought that has not been thought out'. In
his Day for Life sermon Cardinal O'Brien stated 'I can't
change the teachings of Jesus Christ. I can't change the
Ten Commandments. That's what I'm ordained to teach
and to preach: "Thou shalt not kill".' In saying this he was
recognising that Catholicism's teachings may sometimes
be uncomfortable; but, as the 900 hundred pages of the
Catechism of the Catholic Church reveal, what lies behind
them is unquestionably thought that has been thought out.

5.
Sectarianism and culture

The annual Edinburgh Festival is the largest international arts gathering in the world. In the summer of 1999, in the course of an otherwise generally uncontroversial programme, the leading Scottish composer James MacMillan gave a talk entitled 'Scotland's Shame' in which he spoke of 'sleep-walking bigotry' and 'visceral anti-Catholicism' disfiguring the life of an ancient but newly invigorated nation. The next day, and in the following days and weeks, the Scottish, British and international media and press carried discussions of the issues raised by MacMillan, who is himself a Catholic.

Such, indeed, was the row surrounding his claims of religious prejudice and bigotry that the governing coalition in the newly established Scottish Parliament indicated that it would reverse its original decision not to include a question on religious affiliation in the 2001 Scottish national census. The point being that such information would be helpful in trying to ascertain whether, as MacMillan and others have claimed, anti-Catholic prejudice has had an impact on the educational attainment, employment and health of those populations of Irish and other immigrant origins who are, or traditionally have been, overwhelmingly Catholic.

In addition to this political response the Scottish historian Tom Devine, then director of the Research Institute of Irish and Scottish Studies at the University of Aberdeen and author of the *The Scottish Nation* (1999) edited a

volume of essays by academics, writers and church figures
in which the themes of MacMillan's lecture – and the reactions to it – are examined (*Scotland's Shame? Bigotry and
Sectarianism in Modern Scotland* (2000)). What follows
is drawn in large part from my contribution to that
volume; a contribution arising from the fact that MacMillan began his Festival talk by quoting from an article I had
published in the *Catholic Herald* on the eve of the May
1999 elections for a Scottish parliament.

Scottish religious and intellectual history has been
dramatic and powerful. For fifteen hundred years, from St
Columba to John Knox and on to Cardinal Winning, Scottish religious figures have helped shape both the nation
and outsiders views of it. In philosophy, David Hume,
Adam Smith and Thomas Reid all gave birth to ideas that
have influenced the world. And the greatest impact of
Presbyterianism and common-sense philosophy was in
North America, especially in what is now the United
States. The eighteenth-century independence and constitutional debates were contributed to by Scots; and large
numbers of colleges and universities can trace their
origins and educational policies to Scottish religious and
philosophical ideas. In addition, as the MacMillan affair
may show, Scottish experience of politics, culture and religion could be of more than just historical interest.

In the article from which he quoted, I considered the
general standing of the main Christian denominations,
commented on the issue of sectarianism, and claimed that
Catholics could hope to make a significant contribution to
the development of politics and culture in Scotland by
advancing certain ideals. In particular, that of society as a
moral community in which responsibilities stand alongside rights, in which material goods are produced with an
eye to benefit as well as to profit, and in which the value of
life is respected as well as its quality being promoted.
Intellectually and culturally the Catholic contribution
should be to challenge materialism, instrumentalism,
hedonism and short-term gratification.

Quoting from this, MacMillan observed that he had become increasingly aware of the significance of the Catholic influence and inspiration behind his own work as a composer, writing that

> Since childhood I was brought up to deal with reflective abstract concepts like the metaphorical, the metaphysical and the sacramental. In later life there was a thankfully smooth transition of these concepts from the purely religious sphere to the artistic sphere, although these two things are the one and the same for me . . . The Catholic and the artist, at a fundamental level, can understand each other because the origins of their most precious metaphorical concepts are the same.

Since the reports and general reaction to MacMillan's lecture focused on his charges of anti-Catholic bigotry, it is important to note the positive suggestion that the arts might provide a basis on which to establish a dialogue between Catholicism and the wider culture. MacMillan himself returned to the point, remarking that the arts is the one area of Scottish public life in which he had not encountered anti-Catholic sentiment, and suggesting that this may be due to the fact that there is a sense among those working in this area of a need to reconnect with Scotland's artistic (pre-Reformation) past. These ideas set me thinking about the connection between growing up a Catholic and becoming disposed to the aesthetic and to the arts. This has been my own experience and here I relate something of it, highlighting points at which it bore upon my impressions of aspects of non-Catholic Scottish culture.

As a child growing up in the West of Scotland in the 1960s I felt no threat of anti-Catholic sentiment. I was aware of the rivalry between Celtic and Rangers football clubs and their supporters (Catholic and Protestant, respectively) and of the sectarian violence associated with this. But I had no interest in football and rarely saw fans on their way to and from games. Occasionally I witnessed an Orange Lodge Parade, generally through the windows of my father's car as we were held back with the other traffic to let the marchers pass. The impression, I think, was one of physicality and roughness: bodies scrawny or fat, faces pale or flushed, ungainly swaggers, cheap ill-fitting clothes and crudely coloured designs. These reactions seemed to confirm something that I picked up at home, namely the idea that for the most part Protestants were in certain ways unaesthetic, without sensitivity or cultural sensibility, particularly in regard to the expressive and the visual.

This aesthetic – and evidently partial – judgement now seems revealing about my own background and relevant to the question of the place of religion in Scottish culture. At home the sectarianism that characterised inner-city divisions was almost never discussed, even though religion – Catholic *and* Protestant – was a significant formative influence. I was an only child in a quiet and well-ordered home in the West End of Glasgow, Scotland's largest (and most Catholic) city. My mother came from an interesting and gifted Irish family, but not one of those that had emigrated directly to Scotland for reasons of economic necessity. We had no Irish connections and until recently it never occurred to me to think of Ireland as a place that might have special interest for me. My maternal grandfather had served in the Royal Navy from which he retired to settle in Kent in the south east of England.

Growing up there, my mother and her sisters found themselves attracted to the theatre and began to travel and work in Europe where they enjoyed considerable success. Finding herself in Italy at the time of the declaration of war my mother who had dual British/Irish nationality elected to stand by her British identity and paid the price for this by being interned, thereafter remaining in more or less restrictive forms of confinement until the liberation. It was there and then that she met my father who was serving in the RAF, and they were married in Kent at the end of the war.

My father came from a fairly dour Scottish background. An only child of older parents he was raised in the Kirk, his father being a Master of the Masonic Lodge. Living within sight of the Ochil Hills overlooking Stirling Castle and the valley of the River Forth he spent much of his youth walking the glens and ridges. A solitary and sensitive boy he took to drawing and photography. He would have liked to study at art school, but my grandfather would have none of it, thinking such an education to be a waste of time. In retrospect this seems both sad and ironic for my grandfather was no Philistine: an accomplished keyboard player he served as organist in the local Presbyterian church. As was typical, his interest focused on religious music, in particular the choral work of church composers, and I think he cared for little beyond this. My father had been encouraged to learn the piano and in due course this would be a point of shared interest with my mother. By her account, and in my memory he was the better of the two and could carry off the likes of Gershwin's *Rhapsody in Blue*. But he remained largely unpraised by my grandfather who may have resented his son's broader talents and the fact that they were applied more widely than were his own.

On arriving in Scotland my mother had found the gloom very dispiriting. She had thrown herself into parish life and did so again in Glasgow while beginning to build a home there, decorating it far more brightly and with much greater imagination than was common even in middle-class circles at the time. No doubt she was attempting to recreate something of what she had known in Ireland, the south of England and in Italy.

After the death of his wife my grandfather moved in with us for some while and so began an interesting time of our lives. A few years previously my father had converted to Catholicism being received into the Church by a Franciscan, Fr Bonaventure. However my grandfather never knew of this conversion and I believe he may have died in ignorance of it. What he did know, however, was that his

son had married a Papist and that I was being educated at
Jesuit schools. Even so I never remember rows over the
issue of my schooling, though my grandfather used to tell
me that the reason the Pope wore 'long dresses' was to
cover his cloven hooves.

At school I was not particularly academic and chose to
pursue art. The fact that Charles Rennie MacIntosh's
famous Glasgow Art School building was across the street
from the Jesuit college may have been a factor, though at
school-leaving time no other boy was destined for art
school. Most Catholic families were keen to improve their
material circumstances and hence such an option was not
likely to have parental approval, though my own were
entirely supportive, and I think my father was happy to see
me pursue what he had once hoped for himself. We moved
to Kent, where I had long spent my summer holidays, and
I began my art school education. Following this I studied
philosophy and in the last year of my study a post became
available at St Andrews, Scotland's oldest university
(1411). I applied, was surprised to be appointed and with
my wife Hilda returned to Scotland where we have lived
ever since.

The town being closely associated with the Reformation, and the University being thought of as socially elitist
and mostly English there were only three or four Catholics
on the academic staff when I arrived (all of them English).
But I never encountered anti-Catholic bigotry. It was only
some years later when I began writing for the press and
appearing on the radio that I began to receive pointedly
anti-Papist insults and for the most part these came from
correspondents in the West of Scotland!

In 1999 an affair involving a prominent Scottish defence
lawyer named Donald Findlay who was then Rector of the
University (an office combining representation of student
interest and chairmanship of the Court – the board of
trustees) created a major difficulty for St Andrews. On the
one hand as Rector, Findlay had by all accounts served
the student body very well, and there was every reason to

maintain the recent tradition of according outgoing rectors honorary degrees. On the other hand his loutish behaviour following a Rangers victory over Celtic, singing insulting anti-Catholic songs at a time at which Rangers was trying to put its bad sectarian reputation behind it, caused general embarrassment. My own initial reaction was one of anger. Very quickly, however, I came to think that Findlay may have been irresponsible, foolish and vulgar but that the University ought not to revoke the decision to award the degree, at least not without seeing whether he might embark upon a course of social reparation.

I decided to write a piece in the (Glasgow) *Herald* (established in 1783, it is the oldest English-language daily newspaper in the world). Entitled 'A Matter of Honour' this was published on the day that the University Senate was due to discuss the affair and it produced a significant mail both to the paper and to me personally. Among the latter was a particularly abusive letter – from a *Catholic* in the West of Scotland. Though stylishly expressed his accusations were extreme and bordered on the deranged, including the suggestion that I might owe my position at St Andrews to a willingness to serve the Protestant cause.

One defence of 'Findlay's Songs of Hate' as one paper had headlined the story, is that they belong to a tribal ritual now far removed from its anti-Catholic origins and all but empty of its sectarian meaning. Likewise a defence of my spluttering Catholic correspondent is that I had triggered a folk-memory of bigoted oppression. Each might then be excused on grounds of passion. But this is inadequate. Middle-aged men do behave like overwrought juveniles, and not just when they are tired and emotional; but actions occur in contexts and have consequences. The night Findlay misbehaved, a boy wearing a Celtic football shirt had his throat cut and another was shot in the chest by a crossbow. Meanwhile, blinded by his own prejudices, my Catholic correspondent evidently failed to register the content of my article, grossly misrepresenting it and no doubt relaying his twisted account to others.

The Findlay affair, Macmillan's lecture and other events have exposed veins of deeply rooted sectarianism in Scottish society. The country cannot afford immaturity in regard to such matters. There is much arrested development and cultural retardation on both sides of the divide. Growing up is not an inevitable process; it is an imperative that some find difficult to follow but which is all the more necessary for just that reason. Learning social good manners is an important part of that process. So I return to the aesthetic. Generalising, of course, I suggest that whereas Scots of Catholic backgrounds tend to uncritical sentimentalism and are fiery in reaction to perceived or imagined prejudices and slights, those of Protestant background tend to insensitivity and are unyielding in their self-assurance. The first is a defect of superfluity of feeling, the second one of the lack of it. The former is something I recognise in myself, the latter is what was conveyed to me by the sight of the Orange Parades and by my grandfather's lack of response to his son's artistic talents.

There has been much talk in Scotland in recent years of the importance of the arts. Too often, though, this is perceived in terms of tourism; and when art is considered in its own right the art in question is usually literary. There is no doubting Scotland's interest in the written word, but this is a medium whose appeal is to the intellect and to the discursive imagination. What is underdeveloped in Scottish culture is a properly aesthetic sensitivity to the openness to beauty and transcendence especially as these are present in music and the visual arts. Our backwardness in this regard is due, I think, to the Reformation and to what followed it.

In the late medieval and renaissance periods, St Andrews was to Scotland what Oxford and Canterbury were to England: home of its oldest university and ecclesiastical capital of the nation. Being poorer and more remote from the sources of European artistic and architectural innovation it compared less favourably with its southern counterparts even then; but today the historical contrast is marked. Whereas Canterbury Cathedral stands as a proud and enduring witness to the achievements of the Gothic, the cathedral at St Andrews is a ruin only hinting at its glorious past. The medieval and renaissance University buildings have fared better but by comparison they are fewer and less grand than their Oxford contemporaries.

Relative wealth apart, a further factor serves to explain the difference – the Reformation. Prior to 1560 Scotland had a rich tradition of ecclesiastical art and music. Something of the latter has been rediscovered in recent years, but almost nothing remains of church and college art. Among the few exceptions, the more remarkable for the fact that they are without parallel, are the three medieval maces of St Andrews University, the finest of which is that of St Salvator's College (1461).

Though rich in detail, its true accomplishment is its concise expression of a philosophical-cum-theological world-view. No modernist doubts about the orderliness of the world troubled the designer for whom architectural, botanical and human forms are combined in celebration of religion, science and art. The fact that it was made in Paris hardly detracts from the claim of a rich pre-Reformation artistic heritage since its very commission testifies to discerning patronage. Also, human, intellectual and cultural traffic then moved to and fro and the artisan may have been a Scot.

Five hundred years later there is renewed interest in Scotland in imaginative design. In 1999, the year of the new Parliament as well as of MacMillan and of Findlay, Glasgow was UK City of Architecture and Design. These, however, are in general non-representational arts; thus escaping the biblical ban on graven images reaffirmed by the Protestant reformers. There is little doubt, though, that the shift from a theology that embodied religious ideas in visual representations to one that accorded exclusivity to scripture, had a damaging effect on Scottish art.

On the other hand, it may be that the substitution of the verbal for the visual laid the foundations for the Scottish Enlightenment, and for the strong literary tradition that continues to the present day. Likewise, Calvinist preoccupation with duty may have been a major factor in shaping the laudable Scottish concern for politics and public service.

Yet the repressed will return: slowly and by stages the visual arts have recovered. Significantly, though, the subject matter has rarely been chosen for its intellectual interest. From portraiture in the seventeenth and eighteenth centuries Scots stepped gingerly out of doors to paint the landscape and then returned to a domesticated version of this: the flower-based still-life. More radical spirits moved beyond these themes and began to depict charged human situations, but thereby only confirming the deep influence of Calvinistic moralism. The Renaissance never had a chance to influence Scotland's visual culture, and in certain crucial respects Scotland's development was arrested. The situation is recoverable but it will take great effort and more than this generation to close the gap.

What has not been commented upon thus far, however, is that Catholic and Protestant in Scotland now face a common threat prominent in all Western countries: that posed by egoistic, hedonistic materialism, particularly as this grips the souls of younger generations, including artists. Growing up is hard enough without the temptation of infantile regression. That is a lesson for other parts of Britain, for Europe, North America and the West more generally, no less than for Scotland. And each can learn from the trials, tribulations and triumphs of the other. Although politics matters, the challenge for each of these societies is less political than cultural: it is that of how to return their peoples to a sense of life as directed towards the knowledge, the love and the service of God; and in the first instance to bring about some general understanding of what that might involve.

Section II

Popes and other mortals

6.

The death of a prophet and the life of a saint

'Undoubtedly we have entered the preconclave period that comes towards the end of any long pontificate.' So wrote Peter Hebblethwaite in his book *The Next Pope* (1995) in which he also described the main 'runners' for the succession, mentioning but giving no special attention to Joseph Ratzinger. That was in 1994 and Hebblethwaite died while the book was in press. A decade on, many of the runners had also passed away or were too old to be eligible for election.

Hebblethwaite described John Paul as a 'restless angst-ridden man. Reduced to unwonted, unwanted and wholly relative passivity, he feels himself even more "representative" in his sufferings'. In 1981 the Pope was seriously wounded in an assassination attempt, and a decade later further major surgery removed a tumour of the colon 'about the size of an orange'. Subsequent to that he began to decline under the weight of Parkinson's disease and his suffering became the subject of continuing attention. Yet he lived on, sure that a purpose was being served by his resilient longevity. Hebblethwaite recognised this belief, writing that 'he has a sense of being on borrowed time, and feels confirmed in his policies; if he has been spared by Divine Providence, it is surely for some purpose'.

What might that be? Subsequent to Hebblethwaite writing of the pontificate coming to an end John Paul II promulgated four major encyclicals: *Evangelium Vitae* ('The Gospel of Life'), *Ut Unum Sint* ('That They may be

One') both in 1995, *Fides et Ratio* ('Faith and Reason') in 1998, and *Ecclesia de Eucharistia* ('The Church of the Eucharist') in 2003. These are important communications to the universal Church, on the themes of the value of life, ecumenism, philosophy and theology and the sacrament of the Eucharist. The first two have already entered the record as major encyclicals and have been the subject of much discussion within and beyond the Church and even beyond Christianity. They are, and will continue to be seen as textual highlights of his pontificate.

He also made important ecumenical and inter-religious initiatives. In 1999 and in 2001 he travelled to Romania and to the Ukraine, the first visits of a Western pope to predominantly orthodox countries since the great schism of 1054 that divided Christendom East and West. And in the intervening year he journeyed to Israel praying at the national Holocaust Memorial (*Yad Veshem*) and at the Western Wall of the Temple in Jerusalem where he placed a note praying for forgiveness for the treatment of the Jews.

Returning to his responsibilities as Roman Pontiff, John Paul published a number of Apostolic Exhortations addressed to the Church in the main regions of the world: *Ecclesia in Africa* (1995), *Ecclesia in America* and *Ecclesia in Asia* (both 1999), *Ecclesia in Oceania* (2001) and *Ecclesia in Europa* (2003) and in the same year as the last of these published *Pastores Gregis* ('Pastors of the Lord's Flock') an exhortation addressed to bishops throughout the world. But beyond these ecclesial works the Pope increasingly offered the world sight of his own failing condition as testament to the inescapable reality of life's vulnerabilities. In his book *Memory and Identity* (published shortly before his death) and elsewhere, John Paul spoke of the importance of bearing witness to the human condition in its frailty, countering the cult of invulnerability with the unavoidable image of suffering. But in *Memory and Identity* he also spoke of a mystical transformation. What would otherwise be an evil, and appears as such to many, is a path leading to God. Blameless suffering, willingly accepted out of love, transforms the life of the person bringing them to the threshold of eternity. A peace descends of which the world has little understanding. Such was the condition of the Pope even as he lay struggling for every breath. The day of his death drew near but he neither held back nor reached out for it.

Another explanation of his remarkable survival for a decade beyond the imminent demise predicted by Hebblethwaite and several others is the possibility, which I have not seen discussed even among the religious, that he endured in order that another might mature to the point where he could be elected to the papacy, if not in succession to John Paul then following a short intermediate reign. Peter Hebblethwaite would have lamented the passing from the field of his own favourites; but those included people who were caught up in agendas of the past, as to some extent are we all. A remarkable attribute of John Paul, however, was his ability to appeal to youth. They are the future and their leadership may lie with bishops free of 'liberal' insecurities.

Memory and Identity had its origins in conversations held a decade before at the summer residence of Castel Gandolfo. Two Polish philosophers, Michalski and Tischner, invited the Pope to reflect on the wars and tyrannies of the twentieth century, thinking about them from the standpoints of philosophy and history. More recently John Paul had returned to scripts of those conversations to enlarge upon his reflections. The resulting text is cast in the form of a series of chapters each beginning with a composed question, with successive chapters building to a larger account of the meaning of human history, particularly in its dealings with evil.

Philosophical and theological ideas feature but the style is more that of a reflective sermon delivered to students of European history. Previews of the book and reactions to isolated fragments suggested it would be provocative, but that is not the style and taken in context the points are

unsurprising. It has been said that he likens abortion to
the holocaust. The comparison has been made but it is not
his.

John Paul writes that the Nazis and Soviets chose what
lives to value and exterminated those they despised, and
goes on to say that while these regimes have fallen 'there
remains the legal extermination of human beings
conceived but unborn ... decreed by democratically
elected parliaments' (p. 12). Then later he returns to the
theme: being legislated for does not confer moral permis-
sibility. Hitler was elected and given full power by a parliament, invoking which he invaded Europe, established
concentration camps and eliminated millions. In the new
century 'We must question certain legislative choices
made by the parliaments of today's democratic regimes.
The most immediate example concerns abortion laws'
(p. 152).

The points are not that abortion is equal to the holocaust (how could one begin to measure them?) but first,
that law and morality are not the same, and whereas
mankind may write the former, man is not the author of
the latter; and second, that democracies may still perpe-
trate grave moral wrongs. The Pope spoke of present-day
Europe as a 'continent of [moral] devastation'. Contemplating societies now affluent beyond expectation it is
hard to resist the thought that we have built ruins. John
Paul believed in the goodness of mankind but thought we
can only see this if we accept that we are creatures of a
good God.

The book reveals how when shot in May 1981 the Pope
came close to death. He attributed his survival then to the
protection of heaven. Two and a half decades later he still
survived, but the doors of heaven were opening and he was
soon to be gone. I read *Memory and Identity* during the
last weeks of his life, looking up from the page to the tele-
vision screen and comparing the strength of the words
with the frailty of the author who at his final public
appearance could no longer speak. The experience was

humbling as was the sight of the gathering crowds of young people in the area of St Peter's. In his 1979 book *Sign of Contradiction*, adapted from the words of Luke (2:34) and Acts (that Jesus is 'a sign that is spoken against') and Christians a group that 'everywhere is spoken against', John Paul describes the Church as being such a sign. Others spoke of him in the same terms, and certainly the vast scale of the crowds who attended his World Youth Days, many of whose number gathered in Rome to honour his passing, seemed to be in contradiction to the secularism of the age.

The news for which they waited in sadness came in the late evening of 2 April 2005. Sometime after 9.30 p.m. Karol Wojtyla, Bishop of Rome and two hundred and sixty-fourth successor to St Peter died and thereafter faced his final judgement.

Few who believe in such a thing can doubt that the Divine verdict on his earthly life will have been favourable. According to Roman Catholic dogma the act of canonisation is an infallible exercise of the Church's *magisterium* (its divinely granted moral and spiritual authority). So should his successor or some future pontiff pronounce John Paul to be among the saints, then, so far as the Church is concerned, that will be proof positive of Wojtyla's sanctity. Canonisation will come, I am sure, perhaps even within this decade.

So much for the likely verdict of heaven and of the Church on earth. What will historians make of John Paul, and what should we who lived through his pontificate make of him? In 1991 I was in Cracow on the day the ancient Jagiellonian University bestowed an honorary degree upon Margaret Thatcher. The Rector of the University was moved to say that four people had saved Europe from communism and that two of these were Poles: Karol Wojtyla and Lech Walesa; the other pair was Margaret Thatcher and Ronald Reagan.

The contribution of the Pope to the downfall of the Polish regime is a matter of record. George Weigel's

monumental biography *Witness to Hope* has much to say
on this but more remains to be discovered about his role in
the general collapse of Eastern communism. In 1989,
shortly after the fall of the Berlin Wall, Mikhail Gorbachev
had a private audience with the Pope in Rome while en
route to a summit with President George Bush (senior);
the meeting was confirmation of the Pope's contribution,
and later the former Soviet leader described John Paul as
'the highest moral authority on earth'.

More generally, Wojtyla will be acknowledged as an
independent critic of both capitalism and communism.
His opposition to Marxism was widely reported; but relatively little was made of his opposition to free market
liberalism of the sort favoured by many of his right-wing
admirers. John Paul may have been a primary target for
criticism by progressive theologians, post-Christian feminists, pro-choice advocates, and sexual revolutonaries, but
he was no reactionary, social-elitist, racist or misogynist.
Indeed his statements on nuclear weapons and capital
punishment were particularly unwelcome among American neo-conservatives – including Catholic ones. The
combination of natural law ethics, social democracy, and
internationalism; of rigorism in personal life, social
generosity to the needy and oppressed, and constructive
world diplomacy is an unfamiliar blend in US politics,
though one that has developed in response to his example.

American upholders of traditional morality have sometimes been inattentive in their policies to the poor and the
marginalised – particularly those in areas beyond American interest. In his meeting with President George W.
Bush in July 2001, the Pope declared that

> A global world is essentially a world of solidarity. From this
> point of view, America, because of her many resources,
> cultural traditions and religious values, has a special
> responsibility ... A free and virtuous society, which
> America aspires to be, must reject practices that devalue
> and violate human life at any stage from conception until
> natural death.

In a responding statement the President observed, non-commitaly, 'Every nation, including my own, benefits from hearing and heeding this message of conscience.'

John Paul's long-standing antagonism to liberal individualism once seemed idiosyncratic but it anticipated the communitarian challenge (posed by thinkers such as Charles Taylor, Alasdair MacIntyre and Michael Sandel) to a view of the individual in society first fashioned in the eighteenth century in the French and American revolutions. There are, though, two further aspects of his thought and action that should be emphasised.

First, he was by training and inclination a philosopher-theologian. His writings in this area, in particular his book *The Acting Person* (1979), are contributions to an unusual synthesis of the philosophy developed by St Thomas Aquinas in the thirteenth century, and that fashioned by Austrian and German phenomenologists in the late nineteenth and twentieth centuries. This 'personalism' emphasises the value of human beings as subjects of experience and as moral agents, and insists in opposition to earlier (and usually religious) dualisms that our thoughts and deeds are intrinsically conditioned by our embodied nature. For John Paul human beings are not angels in bodies but rational animals.

This understanding is to the fore in the encyclical *Veritatis Splendor* (1993), but it shaped his whole way of relating to humanity in his own person and as priest and successor of Peter. It was also a powerful motivating force in his opposition to abortion, euthanasia and the general culture of death – given timely and timeless expression in the follow-up encyclical *Evangelium Vitae* (1995). Roman documents rarely offer much in the way of philosophical interest. The recent pontificate, by contrast, was distinguished by the number of occasions on which John Paul II philosophised in the course of addressing the Church. In *Fides et Ratio* he took up the question of the nature of philosophy itself and its relation to religion; and thinkers of all stripes have reason to look with care at what he has

to say about the need of the subject to recover what he
terms its 'sapiential dimension' – the search for wisdom.

The second aspect, more important than his philosophical orientation, was his role as a prophet. Like the figures
in Hebrew scripture, John Paul spoke presciently of the
future and will be found to have anticipated and prompted
events and trends. But the religious prophet is not a
fortune-teller. His or her claims derive not from a third-
eye vision of the future but from intense and powerful
scrutiny of the present, and from a religious understanding of the past. The prophet knows better the mind of God
and sees deeper into the souls of men, and is saddened and
fearful of the gap between them. As we move further from
God the need of prophets grows greater, but so too does
resistance to their message.

John Paul was loved and admired; but was also feared and
hated. This is the condition of prophets in times of impiety.
Familiar too is the personal suffering. For years the Pope
endured pain with dignity and heroic virtue. In the last year or
so his condition was pitiable; his body immobilised and his
features stiffened. Although the physical distress was widely
recognised, he was also sorely troubled in heart by the priestly
abuse scandals, hurt and ashamed by fellow pastors who had
grievously abused their offices of care and trust. It was, he
believed, further evidence of the legacy of original sin, whose
marks according to Augustine are a darkening of the intellect
and a disturbance of the passions.

Personal asceticism, apostolic fervour, and fortitude in
the face of bodily and spiritual trials are marks of the
saint. Before canonisation can occur, however, there has
to be an attested miracle unambiguously attributed to the
intercession of the individual. Catholics who pray for the
soul of Karol Wojtyla are also likely to seek his intercession. And before long the sanctity of another great soul
will be recognised.

7.

Where to now for the pilgrim church?

The primary responsibilities of cardinals include advising the pope and assisting him in the government of the Church. When a pope dies they immediately take up that governance themselves, meeting together in Congregation in Rome until the date appointed for the election of a successor. Following the death of John Paul II that date was set as 18 April 2005. According to the prescribed plan, the cardinals celebrated Mass together in St Peter's Basilica in the morning for the intention *Pro Eligendo Romano Pontifice* (of 'electing a Roman Pontif'), and in the afternoon they proceeded to the Sistine Chapel. Having sung together the hymn *Veni Creator Spiritus* ('Come Holy Spirit Creator') various oaths were taken concerning secrecy and election procedures. Next the command *'Extra omnes'* ('all out') was voiced by Archbishop Marini, the Papal Master of Ceremonies, directing those not involved in the conclave to leave the chapel. Thereafter there were no speeches or debates, only prayer and the ballot.

Already, however, the cardinals had been discussing what was needed and who might provide it, and these conversations continued with increasing intensity into the period of the election. As ever, many factors were at work including personal ambitions and rivalries, and conflicting assessments of the past, present and future directions of the Church. It is not unduly idealistic, however, to suppose that by the time the voting began a mood of

genuine resolve had settled upon the company to do the
best for the Church and the world. If they were faithful to
the understanding of the Church's divine foundation and
its providential protection, and to the intent of the
opening hymn, then the cardinals would also have
believed themselves to be assisted by, indeed to be agents
of the Holy Spirit.

What then were the choices facing the electors? Prior to
the event there was no shortage of books discussing the
details and likely dynamics of the process, and canvassing
probable candidates. Peter Hebblethwaite's *The Next
Pope* had been revised and updated by his widow in 2000,
and this was joined by other similar studies such as
Francis Burke-Young's *Passing the Keys: Modern Cardinals, Conclaves and the Election of the Next Pope* (2001)
and John Allen's *Conclave: The Politics, Personalities and
Process of the Next Papal Election* (2002). Where leadership is in question matters of policy cannot be separated
from personalities; but the former take priority and it is in
terms of these that the efficacy of leaders is properly
judged. A church whose membership numbers over a
billion, covers the globe and includes every race and
culture, cannot hope to satisfy every ambition, but it can
try to group them and identify priorities. The main challenges facing the universal Catholic Church in 2005 and
now, are of two sorts.

First, there are those that concern the Church itself as
an institution. Here we might speak of the need of 'reform
and renewal'. Even the most loyal Catholic would have to
acknowledge that a number of problems came to light in
the period of John Paul's rule, even if the causes of some
of them predated his election. These are serious and need
early and sustained attention if further damage is to be
prevented.

The governance of the Church has become over-
centralised, and as in other areas of life bureaucracy seems
to have shifted from being an instrument to becoming an
end in itself. At the level of the individual diocese, priests

feel burdened with paperwork, while at the Roman level there has been a relentless tendency to determine what must be done throughout the world, often without regard to local traditions and circumstances. It is one thing to insist upon universal acceptance of the fundamentals of dogma, but quite another to require conformity in liturgy and in the ways in which local churches deal with the cultures that surround them.

While John Paul travelled the world opening himself to different societies, Roman officials sometimes acted like colonial managers, regarding difference as an eliminable fault. Worse still than the growth of a centralising bureaucracy was the failure of the Church to ensure that clergy (who for many *are* the Church) behave properly. Sexual abuse was the scandal of John Paul's papacy. It began long before him, and it is a recurrent problem within any institution that has dealings with the young and vulnerable. But it is not good enough to say that these sorts of things happen. Precisely for that reason they ought to be guarded against; and it is especially terrible when those who are supposed to bring good, bring evil instead.

John Paul grew up in a world more reticent and less sexualised than ours (recall that he was nineteen when the Second World War began), and this meant that he had difficulty comprehending that sexual abuse by clergy was a major problem. His successors will have no such excuse for failing to recognise the seriousness of the issue and its effect upon the perception of the Church. Time was when the sight of a priest walking into the sunset with his arm around a young boy would have brought a feeling of appreciation; now it would occasion a call to the police.

This brings me to the second area in which reform and renewal are called for: the nature and formation of the priesthood. Appeals continue for the ordination of women. This is simply not going to happen, largely for the reason given by John Paul II. The Catholic Church develops dogma in accord with three factors: *revelation, tradition* and *reason*. Like the Eastern Orthodox it believes that it has no power to depart from the first two of these even when the third may seem to suggest change. In holding fast to this, however, the Church now needs to find other roles for women, not only as nuns, housekeepers, parish secretaries or primary teachers but as leaders and policy makers for the Catholic community.

There are also the issues of vocations, marriage and sexual orientation. The experience of the Anglican Church has resolved even liberal cardinals not to entertain any departure from the idea that sexual activity should be heterosexual and conducted within the framework of life-long marriage open to the having and raising of children. Even so, many priests have been, are and will be homosexual in *orientation*. Since the Church teaches that this is not itself sinful it has to ask why celibate homosexuals should be any less welcome into the priesthood than others.

This issue is one of principle but it also bears upon the vocations crisis, as does the issue of married clergy. John Paul held to the ideal of the priest whose family was his flock; but the world has changed: the flocks are dispersed and the bachelor shepherds are few and far between. The experience of losing priests to marriage has been painful, and it may be time for Rome to look at the practice of the Eastern orthodox who allow men to marry prior to entering the priesthood (not once in), and who reserve the office of bishop to celibates. The Catholic priesthood already includes married clergy converted from Anglicanism. It seems reasonable, therefore, and is not contrary to either scripture or older tradition, to allow married men to enter the priesthood.

Turning to the laity, questions of sexuality recur. No pope is going to approve homosexual activity. What remains to be seen, however, is how the wider world will think of the issue a decade from now. One effect of Muslim immigration into Western Europe may be to reverse the tide of liberalism, in which case the Catholic view may come to be a meeting point between old and new cultures.

If, on the other hand, homosexuality secures general and settled social acceptance then the opposition of the Catholic Church may be tolerated on both sides as is its opposition to divorce.

John Paul's successors may choose to put the issue of contraception within marriage so far into the background as to become an option, preferring instead to argue for the importance of lifelong heterosexual union, not counting the number of its offspring. The use of condoms in the prevention of HIV/Aids may also be removed from front of stage by being treated as an issue not of birth control but as one of disease prevention. This last debate is already running, even among orthodox cardinals, and I doubt that it will be definitively resolved.

The second broad area calling for attention is one marked out by John Paul himself, the fruits of whose work were in evidence in the days leading up to his death and interment. This is the field of cultural evangelisation: reaching out to those beyond the Catholic, Christian and even religious folds. John Paul challenged both Soviet communism and American capitalism and engaged Muslims and Jews in greater dialogue, while encouraging convergence with German Lutherans and Greek and Russian orthodox. In short, he sought an alliance of theists and a reunification of Christendom.

It was a measure of his achievement that Jews grieved for him in Israel while Muslims did likewise in Iran, and representatives of all the world faiths came to his funeral in Rome. But more remains to be done. In the Middle East the Catholic Church is committed to a two-state solution to the Palestinian/Israeli issue and should now put greater pressure on the US to see this implemented, along with a solution to the issue of Jerusalem.

Meanwhile in South America and in Africa there is need for local solutions to the issue of the Church's involvement in political activity. Borne of his experience of communism, and witnessing versions of liberation theology that were indeed Marxist, John Paul was inclined to issue

blanket condemnations and encourage the calling to Rome
of rebels. His successors are likely to have had different
experiences; the threats to justice now come less from
collectivism than from rampant individualism. Pope
Benedict will have to work out a new interpretation of the
social gospel. In doing so, however, he will continue to
insist that the greatest poverty is spiritual and that material improvement is a means to and not a guarantee of
personal fulfilment.

Here stands the issue of western secularisation. In view
of the reaction to the Pope's death it is absurdly premature
to speak of the end of religion in Europe. Even so membership is down and still falling. On one analysis this is due to
unpopular   policies,   particularly   those   concerning
'lifestyles'; but the truth is that even those denominations
that have been accommodating of the sexual revolution
also have lower church attendances. The problem of Christianity in Western Europe is not that of a defeated ideology. The world did not test Christianity and find it
wanting. Rather the countries of Western Europe, most of
which had been ravaged by wars, elected first a series of
socialist administrations that offered material solutions to
human misery, and then preferred to ditch all serious
ideology in favour of consumerism.

The underlying drift in this history is from the transcendent to the mundane, and successive popes have to
find their own means of advancing religion. One group
seemed especially responsive to John Paul's efforts,
namely, young people. In 1985 he called for a World Youth
Day and this led to some two million coming in the millennium year to hear him in Rome. Pope Benedict may lack
the vibrant charisma of his predecessor but he will work
the harder in other ways to reconnect the Church and the
people of Europe. So far as rising generations are
concerned his own first World Youth Day in Cologne in
August 2005 drew some four hundred thousand people
and was notable for the warmth of the reception given
him.

In the aftermath of John Paul's funeral there was a day or two of press recreation, followed by a gathering of notes and briefs in preparation for the Conclave. A few days later a new pontif appeared on the balcony of St Peter's heralded by the words '*habemus papam*' (we have a pope). In thinking about what challenges face him and the Church he had been chosen to lead it is important to see things not just from the perspective of the world but also from that of the Church.

Political leaders are generally people of indefinite elasticity, modifying their shape and adapting to continuously changing preferences. Not so the Bishop of Rome. The very office of St Peter is understood metaphorically to be the rock upon which Christ built his Church and against which he promised the gates of hell would never prevail. That promise depended not upon a willingness of the office's occupants to change with the times but on the requirement that they would hold fast to those truths which were revealed to them and which they have the responsibility to preach to the world.

Commentators often speak of papal candidates as being 'conservative' or 'liberal', 'traditionalist' or 'progressive'. In one sense these titles are irrelevant. The first and second contrasts are political and cultural, respectively, but what the pope, along with every cardinal, bishop, priest and layperson is required to be is orthodox (correct belief). Other things matter but they are secondary. Whether Benedict or any future pope is politically conservative or culturally progressive will influence how he is seem by the media, but from the point of view of the needs of the Church these are at best partial qualifications. If the pope is to meet the challenge of reforming and renewing the Church itself, or that of developing cultural evangelisation, or of doing both, he will have to command the respect of his colleagues.

The sort of man best able to do that is one who is deeply spiritual, committed to the prayer and sacramental life of the Church, intellectually sophisticated, appreciative of the circumstances and needs of the clergy and laity, and in touch with the aspirations of much of the developed world to avoid being drawn into the debased culture of materialism, individualism and pleasure seeking that is the actual result of secularisation. In the person of Joseph Ratzinger the College of Cardinals, not to speak of the Holy Spirit, found such a man.

8.

Gentle man who will rule by the book

On the second day of the Conclave, Tuesday 19 April, I was giving one of a series of lectures at the Gregorian University in Rome. Now situated in the via della Pilotta across a piazza from a former residence of the Royal Stuarts, the Pontifical Gregorian University enjoys an ancient and distinguished history. First established in 1551 by Ignatius Loyola, the founder of the Jesuits, as the Collegio Romano it numbers seventy-two saints and seventeen popes among its alumni and former faculty. Eight of the last eleven popes studied at the 'Greg' and on that account it has a special interest in papal elections.

No one expected a quick conclusion to the Conclave and so I wandered back slowly eastwards to the 'cottage' provided for me at the Irish College close by San Giovanni in Laterano, the home church of the Bishop of Rome. The morning offerings from the Sistine chimney had been black (no pope elected) and in the late afternoon although the smoke was greyish the bells that accompany an election had not pealed and so I settled down to a salad and some excellent white wine.

The telephone rang: '*habemus papam*' ('we have a pope'). I raced down to the Colosseum desperately trying to get a taxi, then begging motorcyclists for a lift. No success; and so I ran down to the Circo Massimo, across the Ponte Palatino, and along the west bank of the Tiber, beside the Santo Spirito hospital, through into Via della Conciliazione and came to a halt in the crowds gathered in

St Peter's Square to await the appearance on the balcony of the new pope.

Notwithstanding the remarks of some commentators the election of Cardinal Joseph Ratzinger as Pope Benedict XVI was far from being surprising, but it was nevertheless a very significant choice for Roman Catholicism. Following the death of John Paul II the Church seemed poised to restore its leadership to Italy, or to reach further afield – beyond the west and perhaps into the southern hemisphere. In either case many hoped it would find someone ready to carry on the programme of outreach and evangelisation that was associated with John Paul II, at least until his illness confined him to Rome. A charismatic public figure, a man of and for the people who would be more concerned to understand than to instruct would do nicely, thank you.

As it is we were given a somewhat reserved northern European intellectual, and less an evangelist than a churchman. Joseph Ratzinger is not, however, an ecclesiastical administrator, he is a theologian engaged with the question of how the Church can be the principal means through which Christ saves souls.

His fundamental thinking is organised around two core ideas. First, that it is the revealed truths of Christianity that set us free on earth and save us in eternity (an idea elaborated most recently in his book *Jesus of Nazareth* (2007) which comprises one volume of a planned two-volume study). Second, that for this revelation to be correctly understood, preserved and made available to successive generations there must be a Church secured from serious error and moral corruption.

The combination of core ideas is a familiar one, once widely shared among Christians of different denominations, who in different ways also subscribed to the idea of infallibility. For biblical Protestants it is the Bible itself that is the sole inerrant source of truth, for the Orthodox and traditional Anglicans inerrancy extends to the Councils of the Church, and for Roman Catholics a further dimension is added by the role of the pope as successor to Saint Peter, upon whom Christ founded his Church.

Ratzinger holds firmly to the Roman understanding, but whereas in earlier generations it seemed that this was most frequently challenged by other Christians, he believes that the deepest enemy of truth originates outside Christianity in secular thinking, and that this corruption of reason is seeping everywhere, including within the churches and even within the Church of Rome.

The corruption in question is relativism: the idea that truth is manufactured rather than discovered, made by humans to remove the discomfort that genuine truth can sometimes bring. When challenged with the idea that one may be a sinner and that one's sins may lead one to eternal loss of self and of God, it is more comfortable to deny that there is sin than to repent and reform.

For nearly a quarter of a century Joseph Ratzinger served as Prefect of the Congregation for the Doctrine of the Faith, the Vatican body charged with the maintenance of religious truth through teaching. That experience strengthened his conviction that some had exploited the spirit of Vatican II not to deepen an understanding and love of truth but to modify and dilute it so as to conform to the preferences of those who were not only *in* the world but *of* it. Much has been said about the pain of those who came under his inspection but he saw many grown proud, and celebrated, in their dissent.

What, then, can we expect to see from Pope Benedict XVI? He will not, I think, try to emulate the apostolic journeying of his predecessor, ally and friend. He will remain more in the Vatican addressing those aspects of the Church that John Paul neglected. Apart from the conspicuous fact that these need attention Pope Benedict will want to deal with them in order to make good the achievements of John Paul. In that sense he will aim to complete work already done rather than to launch out anew.

The matters in question fall into four related areas: Church governance, theological speculation and instruction, priestly formation and religious practice. Who knows how long he may have for the task and what resistance he may meet, but Benedict XVI will aim to reform and renew the Church. Part of this involves purification. He feels deeply shamed and personally disgusted by the revelations of sexual abuse and the failure of bishops to deal with it. In some parts of the world national and regional conferences of bishops and heads of religious congregations and movements will be wondering, and worrying, about what may come their way from Rome.

In somewhat similar vein he will continue the challenge to those employed in Catholic institutions to teach in accord with the faith and morals of the Church. This is sometimes depicted as a desire to impose personal views but that is the opposite of the truth: he will demand loyalty to the teachings of the Church from those who would use the cover of its institutions to pursue their own opinions. Again I would expect to see some action on this front with consequent outrage, particularly in North America.

There has been much talk of the decline in vocations in the West and some have argued that this means accommodating the requirements for the priesthood to the lifestyles of secular society and not looking too hard at how things are going. The Pope's view is that the priesthood is a calling from God and a gift to Him, and its standards and discipline must be of the very highest. Better to have few good priests than many indifferent or even bad ones. There has been an ongoing series of visitations to American seminaries. Unlike previous such exercises these are not to be old boy get-togethers but demanding inspections, and few doubt that several will fail the test. In particular sexual indulgence will not be tolerated, be it heterosexual or homosexual.

Then there is the matter of religious practice. Joseph Ratzinger is an ascetic and pious priest who prays intensely and conducts Mass with devotion. He is also a man of refined taste, and emotional and spiritual sensitivity. Much of the liturgy practised in churches offends both his aesthetic and religious sensibility. In July 2007, he issued the *motu proprio Summorum Pontificum* advising local bishops that given 'the request of the faithful' Masses according to the Missal of 1962 were to be more generally permitted. The 1962 Misssal precedes the liturgical reforms initiated by Paul VI and contains the order of the Tridentine Mass. That has been something of an icon for traditionalists but in the letter accompanying the *motu proprio* direction Pope Benedict emphasised that the increased availability of the Tridentine Mass was not at odds with the imperatives of the Second Vatican Council. The Mass introduced by Paul VI would still be the norm as would the saying of the Mass in the vernacular.

Somewhat at odds with uninformed interpretations of his liturgical directive, and certainly at odds with the 'God's rotweiler' nonsense, there is an aspect of Pope Benedict's years ahead that may surprise and lead to his becoming loved as well as feared. He is a personally gentle man, of quick wit and personal kindness. Now that he has been relieved of the burden of acting as the Church's chief theological disciplinarian he has a chance to let his softer side show. We already saw something of that at the funeral of John Paul II, a fact that contributed to his speedy election. In future I think we will see it more as he rises to the challenge posed by the acclamation of the crowd gathered in St Peter's square and in the streets leading to it: *'viva papa'*.

The death of John Paul II and the election of Pope Benedict gave Catholics and others much to think about. Some commentators have been keen to minimise the significance of the reaction to the former, describing it as case of 'the Diana phenomenon'. The laziness of the thought outdoes the vulgarity of the phrase. The reaction to the death of Princess Diana was to the premature and violent death of an unhappy and tragic character. The response to the dying of John Paul was to the noble end of a heroic figure, one who had exercised immense moral and spiritual authority within and beyond the world of religion.

Secular observers recognised that the late Pope represented something for which there are few parallels: an institution that is very much in the world yet is not wholly of it. A few Catholic commentators seemed to have lost that sense. Oddly they were less absorbed by the sacred and more preoccupied with the mundane. One reason for this was their hope that with John Paul's passing would come an opportunity to press upon his successor a list of preferred policies on some or all of the following issues: sexuality, divorce and re-marriage, early abortion, embryo research, married and women priests, shared Eucharist, acknowledgement of the equality of other churches (and so on).

The very idea that a candidate could be elected who had 'policies' on these matters that might be in agreement with their own, betrayed a worldly preference to see the work of the Church as more political than sacred, together with a conception of papal leadership hardly less presidential than that favoured by the extreme papal monarchists at the time of Vatican I.

When the result of the election became known, less gracious Catholic dissenters remarked that anyone who thought the Holy Spirit guided the process should remember the corrupt popes of the past, or take note of the fact that 'Ratzinger' ('Pope Benedict' was a hard title for them to utter) was old and his health was a matter of concern. Others warned that while he might have got the job he had better not try to use it to maintain existing policies. Time will tell whether he has heeded this warning.

Observers of these commentators may have noticed that they were generally older men and women who had long been complaining about the teachings of the Church under John Paul II. Many had issues of their own, and had hoped to see a time when their own course of life would be confirmed by changed teachings. It is hard in these circumstances not to think of other commentators and critics who spent much time predicting the succession to John Paul II only to pass away some years before him.

By contrast the election of Pope Benedict occasioned celebration among younger, committed and uncomplaining Catholics. In Rome at the Gregorian (Jesuit) and at the Angelicum (Dominican), at the English and Scots Colleges and elsewhere, younger staff and students toasted the Pope's good health and anticipated a forward movement in the Church. In universities and in seminaries many young Catholics are alive to a spirit of renewal in the Church. They do not share the discontent of the commentators-for-change with nowhere now to go.

We have a duly elected Pope and we have a duty of loyalty to him and to the Church he serves. It is time for the complainers to move on, hopefully reconciling themselves to the will of the conclave; and if they cannot do that then they should at least stand aside and practice dignified restraint. The positions that now need to be considered are *theirs*. The future of the Church is with the young. There is a gap in generations resulting from the turmoil in the Church, to which the dissenters were often contributors, in consequence of which a number of positions are now passing from people in their sixties and seventies to others in their thirties and forties.

The effects of this succession will begin to be felt in this decade, but their fruits lie further in the future. If one were to adopt the language of the sociologists, it would be tempting to say that one must recognise that there will always be decay spots amid growth as the dwindling number of disaffected huddle together to resist a revivified Catholic culture. As has always been the Church's message, however, one should add that it is never too late to return to the fold, and the gift of a new shepherd is a good time to do so.

9.

Street fighter for God

The death of Cardinal Winning, Archbishop of Glasgow, on 17 June 2001 (the feast of Corpus Christi) came as a great shock notwithstanding that he was seventy-six and that he had had a heart attack the previous week. Such was his vitality and presence that it was easy to imagine that he would remain in office for a number of years. Indeed, he was taking a keen interest in the diocesan five-year plan on the day of his discharge from hospital. As it is, however, his death left a significant gap in the fabric of British public life, and a major one in that of the Roman Catholic Church in Britain. The number, source and manner of expressions of appreciation delivered in the hours following his death offered testimony to this.

Archbishop O'Brien of St Andrews and Edinburgh, then vice-President of the Bishops Conference of Scotland (who would later himself receive a cardinal's cap) described Winning as 'a giant among Church leaders, and in many ways the voice of Christianity in Scotland'. The then First Minister in the Scottish Parliament, Henry McLeish, spoke of '[Winning's] sense of pride in his country, his enthusiasm for life, his continued concern for the ordinary people of Scotland and – perhaps above all – his down-to-earth sense of humour'. Lord Steel, then as Sir David and as Presiding Officer of the Parliament, noted that Winning would be remembered 'for his robust contributions to public debate' and for trying 'to lift the eyes of Scots from our own problems to the Third World'. The contemporary

Secretary of State for Scotland, Helen Liddell, spoke of him as 'a man of great vision and immense social conscience ... particularly concerned by the problems of poverty and working tirelessly to help those in most need'. From Westminster Cardinal Murphy-O'Connor singled out Winning's 'humour, dedication, utter loyalty and unstinting defence of the Catholic Church'. The Queen cited his 'very distinguished contribution to the Catholic Church in Scotland and to Scottish public life over many years' and noted that 'he will be much missed'. Downing Street observed his 'strong moral leadership and commitment to social justice [and] his energy, commitment and passionate defence of the core values of the Catholic Church and faith'; and in a personal statement the then Chancellor of the Exchequer Gordon Brown said 'Cardinal Winning will be sorely missed. He was a great Scot and a great Christian. I was proud to know him and his great achievements will be remembered for many years to come.'

His combination of religious fidelity and social conscience were similarly praised by Liberal Democrat, Scottish Nationalist and Conservative leaders, by the Chief Rabbi of the British Commonwealth Jonathan Sacks (who spoke of him as 'a man of principle and moral courage who never bent his messages to the wind of political correctness'), the Moderator of the Church of Scotland and other religious figures north and south of the border. This, too, was the theme of the Pope John Paul's message to the Catholic Church in Scotland: 'This zealous pastor encouraged the communities he served in faith and Christian living, and was particularly outstanding in defence of life and commitment to the poor.' Without question, Scotland without Winning is a poorer country, and perhaps one without a universally recognised Christian voice.

The fifty-three years of his priesthood saw enormous changes in the economy and culture of Scotland and in the position of Catholicism within the nation. The circumstances of his own upbringing, his quickness of wit, strength of will, and lack of pretension all endeared him to the straight-talking, no-nonsense people of the West of Scotland and induced universal respect, if not affection, from politicians nurtured in the same rigorous environment. More significantly, perhaps, Winning made friendships across the range of politics and across the breadth of the country. As a man of the political left it is perhaps unsurprising that he should have been admired by the likes of the sometime Communist union leader Jimmy Reid, or by the former Secretary of State for Scotland John Reid; but Winning also liked, and was liked by, the nationalist leader Alex Salmond and by the Conservative Lord James Douglas Hamilton. These last three were, I think, the major Scottish politicians for whom he had most time.

On the religious front, Winning had the satisfaction of seeing Catholicism move from the position of being regarded as alien, sinister and superstitious to that of being viewed by many as the major form of Christianity in Scotland. Those informed of the minutiae of denominational difference overlook the fact that for the unchurched, who have no background nor special interest in institutional religion, the Christian faith may come to be identified with a contemporary individual and his or her actions and pronouncements. For many in Scotland beyond the diminishing enclaves of Orange Order Protestantism, Winning, and ipso facto, Roman Catholicism was 'the Christian Church'. This was a cause of both humility and excitement for the Cardinal who recognised the power of his position and often sought to exercise it on behalf of specifically Catholic moral and social teachings as well as for the sake of general Christian charity.

Thomas Joseph Winning was born and raised in industrial Lanarkshire, now part of Scotland's 'rust belt'. He was the first of two children of a family of Irish Catholic extraction. His mother was one of sixteen children and was a model of traditional piety. His father had been a coal miner, but having returned from the trenches of the First World War to find himself without employment he set about making boiled sweets which he sold door to door. The difficulty in finding work was due in part to anti-Catholic bigotry which Winning Junior encountered on his daily walks to St Patrick's Primary School, Shieldmuir and later to Our Lady's High School, Motherwell. Thereafter he embarked on training for the priesthood at a series of seminaries: St Mary's College, Blairs in Aberdeen, St Peter's in Glasgow and Mill Hill in London. In 1946 he was selected as one of the first group of students to attend Scots College Rome, recently reopened after the war. There he acquired the Italian language and a liking for its food and culture. Typically, though, his allegiance to West of Scotland pieties was undiminished and he honed his Italian by translating football reports on the performances of Glasgow Celtic – some say entering the Latinised names of its team members into the litany of saints.

Evidently bright, though not conspicuously intellectual or bookish, Winning graduated from the Gregorian in 1949 with the Licentiate in Sacred Theology. He returned to Scots College the following year and began to study Canon Law, receiving the DCL in 1953. Five years previously he had been ordained for the Diocese of Motherwell, and on coming back to Scotland after his Roman education he began a series of parish and diocesan appointments. By 1961 he was back in Rome as Spiritual Director of his old college where he remained for five years becoming along the way an Advocate of the Roman Rota. This latter training equipped him for the office of Tribunal and Vicar Episcopal for Marriage in the Motherwell Diocese, a position he held from 1966 until 1970 when he was appointed first President of the newly created Scottish National (Marriage) Tribunal. Such were the changing times and circumstances that annulment was becoming an issue of more than academic legal interest. While faithful to the Church's teachings on the indissolubility of marriage Winning was appreciative of the difficulties in which people found themselves and he did much to humanise the process of interview and investigation. Then as later he was attentive to the distinction between objective values and principles and subjective circumstances, recognising this to be essential to sound moral theology and to pastoral practice.

Winning's appointment to the Tribunal was due in part to Archbishop Scanlan of Glasgow in whose diocese the office was based. His relocation from Motherwell then allowed Scanlan to secure Winning's nomination as his Auxiliary. From 1971 to 1974 Winning served as Vicar General of the Glasgow Diocese and as parish priest of Our Holy Redeemer, Clydebank, nearby to the shipyard that was, by then, a site of industrial turmoil. Although Winning castigated some of the workers' leaders for their ideological communism he was strongly supportive of the rights of employees to representation and to fair terms of employment. On Scanlan's retirement in 1974 Winning succeeded him and brought to the position a reforming zeal and a liking for direct, unfussed plain dealing. His aims were not bureaucratic but pastoral. Having breathed the spirit of the Vatican Council and seen the effects of decentralised post-conciliarism in some European dioceses he sought to realise these in the city that was home to Scotland's largest Catholic population.

Like Chicago, Glasgow is ethnic, feisty and plain-speaking, and Winning had about him something of the handsome priest-hero of an older style of American family film. Yet like many a film star he was physically smaller than his screen image suggested. As the city underwent a post-industrial make-over and acquired the slogan 'Glasgow Smiles Better', Winning's grin seemed well-suited to the circumstance. A tribute to his man-of the-people status is paid by the story that he was once approached by a Glaswegian who praised him saying 'Whit I like about you is that you hae nae dignity'. While willing to deploy the authority of office, particularly in diocesan matters, Winning was in no way pompous and he was well liked by men who found him companionable, and by women who felt the attraction of his warmth.

As part of his pastoral plan Winning introduced various educational and spiritual initiatives along with a diocesan newspaper carrying the city's motto 'Flourish'. These and similar projects enjoyed mixed fortunes, and their economic cost, together with a lack of interest in the tedious but necessary details of financial administration, contributed to a considerable diocesan deficit. In due course, however, with better management and additional loyal support from the laity this debt was cleared. What in the case of others might have established a black mark was, if anything, viewed as evidence of having one's heart in the right place – that being the kingdom of heaven and not the bank.

Winning was widely and rightly perceived to be accessible and passionate with no time for impenetrable spin-doctoring. These qualities endeared him to his loyal staff though they also caused occasional difficulties calling for subsequent diplomacy. There were also times of real pastoral difficulty arising from the elopement of Bishop 'Roddy' Wright of the Western Isles, and from cases of sexually abusive priests. He found it hard to deal with such problems in part because he could not altogether comprehend them. Also he made the understandable mistake of assuming that when a fellow bishop told him that he had not had an affair and fathered a child, or when one of his clergy denied that they had abused children, they could be believed. Winning never quite got over these deceits or the chronic wrong-doing they concealed.

Following his appointment as Archbishop, Winning quickly moved from being a regional to a national and then international figure. He was, in sequence, President of the Scottish Bishops' Conference Justice and Peace, Social Welfare and Education Commissions, and President of the Conference itself from 1985 to his death. He served in the Sacred Congregation for the Doctrine of the faith (1978–84) and on the Bishops' Conferences of the European Union and of Europe more generally. In 1994 the Pope elevated Winning to the College of Cardinals and a tartan army of some fifteen hundred Scots followed him to Rome

for the receipt of the scarlet cap. If this was a mark of
Winning's popularity, it was also a tribute to his identifica-
tion with the people. Remarkably, he met every incoming
Scottish flight at Leonardo da Vinci airport, greeting his
folk – Catholic and otherwise – into the small hours. He was
only the third Scottish Cardinal since the Reformation and
only the second to reside in Scotland itself.

Winning's official positions established the need, and
provided additional opportunities, for him to speak out on
a range of moral and social issues. He was neither reticent
to do so nor unsure of what to say. Among the targets of
his criticisms were Latin American dictatorships; the
policy of nuclear deterrence; the Thatcher Government's
welfare policies; the Falklands and Gulf wars, the 1701 Act
of Settlement (preventing a Catholic ascending to the
throne or the heir or sovereign marrying a Catholic); the
'woolly theology' of the Prince of Wales, the alliance of
secular and Kirk opposition to Catholic schools; the 'sham'
of Tony Blair professing personal opposition to abortion
but voting to permit it, even up to birth in certain circumstances; the UK policy of allowing cloning of human
embryos; the repeal of sections 28 and 2A prohibiting the
promotion of homosexuality; and the New Labour government's policy on asylum seekers.

Winning expressed himself in a variety of ways, some
planned and crafted others spontaneous and unguarded.
His willingness to speak on matters of deep contention
and to do so in terms that all could understand led to the
tag 'Cardinal Controversy' being applied by the press, but
unlike some figures he was not an obsessive self-publicist
and he did not seek to unsettle but to confirm Christian
orthodoxy. No doubt greater prudence might have made it
harder for his opponents and critics to misrepresent him
as a reactionary bigot. The fact, however, is that the metropolitan cultural environment is increasingly anti-Christian and it is naive to suppose that accommodation will
serve to protect Catholic interests and values, let alone
persuade others to embrace them.

For anyone who took the trouble to read his more developed statements, such as in his *Spectator* essay 'Why I Must Protest' (10 June 2000), or his *Herald* article 'Are we Making Strangers Welcome?' (1 June 2001) in which he roundly castigated his fellow Scots for criticising asylum seekers and overlooking the extent of their own immigrant past, it was clear that Winning's immediate reactions were securely rooted in a coherent and well-articulated moral theology. The central pillars of this were the principles of beneficence, of non-maleficence and of equality: do good, do no evil, and treat each person according to their intrinsic value.

At the opening of the Scottish Parliament there was a rendition of Robert Burns' song 'A Man's A Man for A' That'. This tribute to the equality of human dignity beneath the surface of soil and circumstance, written in 1795, is close to Winning's own passionate feeling for the oppressed:

> Is there for honest Poverty,
> That hings his head, an' a' that;
> The coward slave we pass him by,
> We dare be poor for a' that!
> For a' that, an' a' that.
> Our toils obscure an' a' that,
> The rank is but the guinea's stamp,
> The Man's the gowd [gold] for a' that.

Having been something of an 'Old Labour' man, in later times Winning strongly favoured devolution and even tilted towards the Scottish Nationalist's aspiration to independence. He did so in part for immediate advantage in relation to matters such as Catholic schools, which the Nationalists went so far as to celebrate, but also because he believed the new centrist politics was largely opportunistic, unprincipled and directed towards satisfying material and hedonistic interests. More broadly, however, he saw in the idea of 'Scotland in Europe', as he put it in a much quoted speech, a possible realisation of the ideal of subsidiarity and the prospect of reintegration of a once Presbyterian and now increasingly irreligious society within the historic heart of Western Christendom.

Winning was a romantic idealist whose hopes were not idle dreams but expressions of a commitment to Christian values and a conviction that in God's good time and through our endeavours the values of the Kingdom might be more extensively embraced. In the central Scotland of his childhood a Catholic might easily expect to be discriminated against, socially excluded and even physically assaulted. Notwithstanding the sectarian bigotry highlighted in James Macmillan's account of 'Scotland's Shame', the fact of the matter is that Catholics now take their place in society, and some – such as Thomas Winning – even manage to be leaders of it.

In advancing the Catholic cause, however, he was not mindless of the fine historical and continuing contribution of the Kirk. On the day he died he was due to have delivered a sermon at Burntisland parish church. It was there in 1601 that the General Assembly of the Church of Scotland met with King James VI in attendance and proposed the idea of the retranslation of the Bible. Ten years later the Authorised version was published. Winning's words were read to the congregation to whom word of his death only arrived later:

> As a cardinal of the Roman Catholic Church I do not hesitate to give thank for the beauty, the power and the language of the King James bible ... Here in Burntisland four centuries ago, a very significant step was taken in building a Christian civilisation which has weathered the storms of the years. But that storm still rages, and our society needs to hear God's word and be challenged by the values of God's kingdom and the person of Jesus Christ.

Thomas Winning preached those words both in and out of season, and he challenged new orthodoxies as well as old heresies. Scotland is a better country for his life and work and was a poorer one for his passing.

Afterword

Subsequent to the publication of the foregoing appreciation (originally in the *Tablet*), the then Moderator of the
General Assembly of the Church of Scotland wrote to the
magazine to say that 'Haldane's estimate of the Scottish
Christian Church risks the continuation of the sectarian
rivalry which has so bitterly scarred the face of Britain and
Europe for centuries' (7 July 2001). This comment came
as a surprise. It was unfortunate to have a tribute made the
subject of controversy, the more so since readers of my
article generally received a quite different impression to
that suggested by the Moderator's letter.

His criticism was based on a single sentence 'For many
outside the diminishing enclaves of Orange Order Protestantism, Winning and ipso facto Roman Catholicism, was
"the Christian Church".' By way of response he then
commented that 'Among [the other Christian Churches in
Scotland] are the 600,000 adult members of the Church of
Scotland, ill characterized by Professor Haldane as "the
diminishing enclaves of Orange Order Protestantism".'

That, however, fails to acknowledge the sentence immediately prior to the one quoted, which obviously provides
the proper context for it. I wrote

> For the unchurched, who have no background or special
> interest in institutional religion, the Christian faith may
> come to be identified with the actions and pronounce-
> ments of a contemporary individual. For many outside the
> diminishing enclaves of Orange Order Protestantism,
> Winning and ipso facto Roman Catholicism, was 'the
> Christian Church'.

My point was neither sectarian nor triumphalist, but an
assessment of the popular perception. I hold to this and
offer as evidence the press and media coverage arising
from the Cardinal's death, which, as the Moderator must
have known, was quite without precedent for a churchman. On the day of the funeral for over two hours BBC

Scotland carried the entire service live, preceded and succeeded by assessments and commentaries. It certainly promoted the event as a national one and there is no other church figure in Scotland of any denomination whose passing would be treated in these ways.

So far as the matter of 'the diminishing enclaves of Orange Order Protestantism' is concerned it is surprising to imagine that I meant by this regular members of the Church of Scotland. The Orange Order reviles the Catholic Church and stands opposed to the ecumenism of the Kirk. The day after publication of the Moderator's letter the *Sunday Herald* carried several reports and commentaries on sectarianism occasioned by an interview with Jack Ramsay, Grand Secretary of the Grand Orange Lodge of Scotland in which he was quoted as follows: 'The Roman Catholic Church is the MacDonald's of religion . . . it wants to spread its influence. We need a bulwark against it. The Church of Scotland is too weak and unwilling to do that.'

In a number of articles and broadcast interviews I have made clear my admiration for the Kirk and for its good influence within Scotland (also its indirect influence in my own life, my father having been a convert from it). James MacMillan began his Edinburgh Festival talk on 'Scotland's Shame' by quoting one such article 'A Nation Under God' (see chapter 5. *Sectarianism and Culture* above) in which I wrote as follows: 'So long as they proceed with delicacy, and especially with respect for the Kirk, which has often been a benign force in Scottish society, Catholics can hope to make a significant contribution to the development of politics and culture.' More to the point perhaps I ended my appreciation by writing 'In advancing the Catholic cause, however [Cardinal Winning] was not mindless of the fine historical and continuing contribution of the Kirk' and went on to give the example of the sermon in praise of the King James Bible which he was due to deliver in Burntisland Kirk the day he died. I hope that the then Moderator re-read the original article, and that in doing so he saw it anew.

10.

Three nineteenth-century liberals

The Scots philosopher David Hume wrote in 1757 of 'the durable admiration which attends those works that have survived all the caprices of mode and fashion, all the mistakes of ignorance and envy'. Unquestionably his own writings have passed outstandingly the 'test of time'. As one moves forward to the present, however, the test is necessarily harder to apply. Even so, one may ask of the nineteenth century what works and writers have survived and are likely to endure. So far as philosophical and reflective writings are concerned two figures stand out undiminished by the passage of time: John Henry Newman and John Stuart Mill. Many might regard these as not merely contrasting but opposing figures. Certainly there are significant differences between them, but there are also points of similarity and agreement that ought to be observed. This I will do, but I also wish to introduce a third contemporary intellectual who, though his name is now far less well known, shared something of their educational concerns, and who has a legacy that also stands undiminished.

Newman and Mill were born within five years of one another, in 1801 and 1806, respectively, but Newman was the longer lived, dying in 1890 to Mill's 1873. Their lives had points of resemblance. Both were London born, the first sons of middle-class families. Both took to solitary and serious reading early in life; both wrote voluminously with everything from academic studies to newspaper articles; both were great letter writers.

Both challenged the expectations of their times: Newman by his conversion to Roman Catholicism, Mill by his agnosticism and advocacy of women's rights. Both were concerned with the nature and value of education, and both made major contributions to a tradition of thought and practice that is in danger of being lost sight of, namely liberal perfectionism – not the vulgar contemporary notion of liberty as indifference or relativistic laissez faire, but rather the principle that freedom is a necessary element in the objective, universal good of self-realisation.

Mill's father, James, was born in Montrose in 1773 the son of a cobbler. With the support of Sir John Stuart of Fettercairn (after whom J. S. was named) James Mill went to Edinburgh University where he attended the moral philosophy classes of Dugald Stewart, one of the later figures of the Scottish Enlightenment. At first intending for ministry in the Kirk, James moved to London, to journalism, and into agnosticism.

In London he joined the circle of radicals that included the Edinburgh born and educated Henry, later Lord, Brougham, the utilitarian Jeremy Bentham and the economist David Ricardo. James Mill's own contribution to the development of thought was through his popularising of the ideas of Bentham and Ricardo; his part in arguing the case for wider access to university, and the education of his son, John Stuart.

Together with the other philosophical radicals, Mill senior played a role in the establishment in 1826 of University College London, where John Henry Newman's youngest brother Francis served for twenty years as Professor of Latin. They were also supportive of the Mechanics Institute that was to become Birkbeck College, named after the Yorkshire born but Edinburgh educated George Birkbeck, whose own first employment had been at the Andersonian Institute in Glasgow.

The Scottish commitment to education was also directed domestically, and John Stuart was homeschooled. By his own account, the rigour and rigidity of that education – learning Greek word lists at three years old, reading Aesop, Herodotus and Plato by the age of eight, then adding Latin, as well as history, algebra and logic, followed by philosophy and economics – gave him a twenty-five-year head start on his contemporaries, but also induced a nervous breakdown by the age of twenty-one.

Newman, too, collapsed about the same age through the weight of academic studies, and took only a third-class degree at Oxford. Such was the recognition of his brilliance, however, that the following year he was offered a fellowship at Oriel, then the best of the colleges; an event he described as 'the turning point in my life, and of all days most memorable'.

Each was to write many fine books, and each knew the work of the other. Newman studied and was certainly influenced by Mill's *Logic*; while Mill read with care several of Newman's works on the Early Church and on Christian belief. They had, of course, taken different paths and stood quite some distance apart; but interestingly in those writings likely to be most enduring, and in which they address themes of broad public interest, there is a kind of convergence, and it is here especially that they have things to teach us about the meaning and value of human freedom, and the means of communicating it to rising generations.

Mill is principally associated with *On Liberty* (1859) and *Utilitarianism* (1861). The general assumption is that the first praises freedom over constraint, and is thereby a founding text for state neutrality in matters of the conduct of life. Likewise, the second is easily presumed to say that moral worth lies entirely in producing the greatest happiness of the greatest number.

In fact, however, Mill's understanding of freedom is not that of the neutralist. On the contrary he thinks that the point of liberty is to enable people, individually and collectively, to perfect themselves in accord with their true human nature. Freedom is not aimless, it has a definite direction: human goodness, but it is part of the value of that goal that it is chosen not coerced. Likewise, while Mill certainly values happiness, it is *virtuous* happiness not mere satisfaction he has in mind, and morality is as much about character as outcome. As he writes: 'it matters not only what men do but what manner of men they are that do it'.

Newman is an advocate of conscience and liberty of thought but is careful to distinguish these from mere 'free thinking' or relativism. In his *Apologia* (1864) he writes 'Liberty of thought is in itself a good; but it gives an opening to false liberty' by which he meant the claim of an individual to be able to judge everything by his own lights. He also explored the difference between mere opinion and disciplined thought in his work *On the Idea of a University* (1852).

That study is now commonly regarded as the greatest piece of sustained thinking about the nature and value of university education. Fittingly, Mill turned his own mind towards the purposes of higher education when he gave his inaugural address as Rector of St Andrews in 1867. Like Newman he emphasises the formation and continuing exercise of the mind, the development of conscience and the cultivation of aesthetic sensibility, seeing that the practice of these is part of liberal virtue. These activities and the values associated with them might nowadays attract the description 'elitist education' and there is an obvious sense in which both men were elitists, but they saw a connection between the cultivation of intellectual excellence and the development and practice of moral virtue.

Herein enters my third figure. In his biography of Cardinal Newman (1912), Wilfred Ward describes Newman's attitude to others who, like him, were concerned with the threat to Catholicism posed by what Ward describes as 'the Anti-Christian tendency of contemporary "Liberalism"'. 'Liberalism' is put in quotes to indicate that the perspective in question was far from liberal in Newman's sense. It was also, in the French variant with which Ward was concerned, a viewpoint more hostile to religion than was Mill's own. Ward then writes that

> [Newman] was keenly in sympathy with the general aims of such men as Montalembert, Lacordaire, and Frederic Ozanam, who regarded it as the great need of the times that the Catholic Faith should be explained in such a way as to appeal to the educated classes among their contemporaries.

Later Ward quotes the last of these as writing that the ideal of the 'Liberal school of Catholics' is 'to seek in the human heart all the sacred cords which can reunite it to Christianity, to re-awaken in it the love of truth, justice, and beauty, and then to manifest in revealed faith the ideal of these three things to which every soul aspires'. This ideal recalls Newman's own and it may have inspired his ongoing efforts at reconciling faith and reason.

Who then was the admired advocate of liberal Catholicism? 2007 saw the tenth anniversary of the beatification of Frederic Ozanam, founder of the Society of St Vincent de Paul. Ozanam's life was relatively short; born in 1813 his health declined while he was still in his thirties and in 1853 he returned to France from Italy where he had gone in hope of a cure. He died that year in Marseille, leaving behind his wife Marie Josephine and their eight-year-old daughter Marie.

In his forty years, the Blessed Frederick achieved a great deal both as a scholar and teacher, and as a friend of the poor and needy. Intellectual life was part of his heritage. The family had Jewish origins but had converted to Catholicism in the seventeenth century. His great-granduncle Jacques was a brilliant mathematical prodigy who in his youth had developed an addiction to gambling which he later overcame. His reputation among mathematicians was established in his lifetime and endures to the present day, but he was also known to his contempo-

raries for his religious faith and his charity to others. He is
reported as saying that 'it is for the scholars of the
Sorbonne to dispute; for the Pope to decide, and for a
mathematician to go to heaven in a perpendicular line'.

Jacques' combination of scholarship, piety and Christian charity was repeated in the life of his great-grand
nephew. Frederic began his academic work early, writing
about the ideas of those French radicals who argued that
the needs of the people demanded not only revolutionary
politics but the elimination of religion. The French Revolution of the decade 1789 to 1799 had overturned the
monarchy, the aristocracy, and the feudalism that went
with them; but it had also targeted the Catholic clergy as
also enjoying social privileges, and as being, in the eyes of
the revolutionaries, peddlers of superstition. The glorious
future was to be republican and secular.

In fact it proved despotic and brutal. In an eleven-
month period between 1793 and 1794 which came to be
known as '*la Terreur*', some 30,000 people were killed in
mass executions by guillotine. The memory of this was still
fresh when Ozanam was born, and he himself witnessed
two further periods of social violence in France, the July
revolution of 1830 challenging a restored monarchy, and
that of 1848 which put an end to monarchy replacing it
with the (short-lived) Second Republic. Frederic agreed
with the radicals that the poor of the cities suffered terri-
bly and that there needed to be social justice, but he also
believed that their suffering was spiritual as well as bodily
and that they needed religious as well as material goods.

As in the Britain of Mill and Newman, economic and
technological developments had brought people from the
countryside into the cities, producing unimaginable physical squalor and terrible moral degradation. Violence and
abuse were rampant; disease and starvation brought sick-
ness and early death. Ozanam perceived that the situation
was terrible but he also viewed the revolutionaries' solution as hopelessly utopian and dangerously Godless, a
'cure' more fatal than the disease. In response he was

challenged to offer an alternative, and in reply in 1833 he and seven others established the Confraternity of Charity. One year later this had a hundred members, and in 1835 he reconstituted the group as the Society of St Vincent de Paul, named after another Frenchman who in the early 1600s had founded the first 'conference of charity' for the assistance of the poor, and had established such groups throughout France where they flourished until, ironically, the French Revolution.

Following the death of his parents Frederic considered a vocation but decided in favour of an academic career securing a position as a professor of literature at the great Paris university La Sorbonne. Thereafter he combined intense and fruitful commitments to scholarship, to spiritual development and to charity. In his mid twenties he wrote an important work on Dante and Catholic thought, and a decade later another major study of Christian civilisation in the Middle Ages. Besides these he wrote about German culture, and his last work was on the theme of pilgrimage in Spain.

Frederic Ozanam's life was divided between devotion to God, care of his family, service to the needy, and academic scholarship. He combined these last two in a way that challenged those who elevated social revolution and disparaged religious belief. Far from faith being at odds with intellectual enquiry, and devotion being at odds with practical concern, Ozanam showed that they are complementary: belief seeks completion in understanding; and love of God seeks completion in service to his children. Frederic wrote that

> Those who wish no religion introduced into a scientific [i.e. scholarly] work accuse me of a lack of independence. But I pride myself on such an accusation ... I do not aspire to an independence, the result of which is to love nothing and to believe nothing.

Ozanam also wrote that he had laid the foundations of the Society of St Vincent de Paul in order to 'insure my faith with works of charity'. This is a profound thought but easily misunderstood. He did not mean that he was taking out a spiritual insurance policy in case his faith failed, hoping that his good works would then save him. Rather he was pointing to the fact that the Christian virtues of faith, hope and charity are interrelated and mutually reinforcing. To the extent that I lack one, so I lack the others; and to the extent that I am strengthened in one so I am strengthened in others.

The philosophers of the ancient world identified four cardinal virtues: prudence, temperance, justice and courage. Each is a disposition to act in certain ways in reaction to particular kinds of situation, and the aim of a good Greek or Roman education would be to cultivate these virtues, forming habits of choice and response by which one might attain (and retain) various goods that contribute to human fulfilment.

The Christian virtues of faith, hope and charity also incline to human well-being and completion, but on the supernatural level, i.e., in relation to our spiritual nature and destiny. Each virtue is a gift from God, but each also requires our co-operation and our effort to strengthen it in our lives. Faith reveals what our last end is, and keeps us on track towards it. Hope tells us that that spiritual end is neither assured nor impossible. We may be confident that heaven is open to us, but that confidence is based on the gift of grace, for by itself human effort is insufficient to lift us out of sin, and free us of its effects.

Writing in the *Confessions*, St Augustine says that the two principal natural effects of original sin are the darkening of the intellect and the disturbance of the passions. Every individual, every family, every society, every generation can see evidence of these. We know we go wrong and that by ourselves we cannot escape ignorance, stupidity, intemperance and over-indulgence. We sense the possibility of something better but we recognise our own inability to achieve it. A natural estimate of the situation would counsel despair, but a religious understanding turns to hope – not optimism, but a belief that however bad it gets there is the possibility of recovery, of redemption and even of fulfilment.

Christian charity is not a 'telethon' spirit of generosity, but, first, a love of God as creator of all that is good, and, second, a love of our neighbour for God's sake. Sentimentalism encourages us to suppose that everyone is lovable; Christian charity teaches that, lovable or not, everyone should be loved as sons or daughters of God. Such charity is not simply self-sacrifice or generosity, let alone complacency or indifference towards sin, for all of these may be directed to bad as well as good ends. Rather it is a love of persons, not the mass of mankind, nor those whom we choose to love, but each and every individual as a creature and child of God.

'Faith, hope, love abide, these three; but the greatest of these is love' (1 Corinthians 13:13). St Paul's words are not a witness to human sentiments or achievements but a testament to divine gifts. We cannot create them but we can develop and deploy them; and we offend God if having been given them without merit or effort, we reject or squander them. These virtues are central to human life and without them we would perish; but they are not mere abstract theological treasures. Rather they are vital powers by which we can live and help others to live. That is what the young Frederic Ozanam recognised in reflecting on the deprivations of the poor and the revolutionary programmes of the radicals. Without the Christian virtues mankind perishes but with them great things are possible.

The confraternity established by Frederick Ozanam and seven associates in 1833 has grown over the last two centuries into a movement that has well over half a million members, and is active in one hundred and thirty-five countries across five continents. In his own day Ozanam's Christian fellowship seemed tiny and fleeting against the forces of secular progressivism. Yet today the French revolutionaries against whom he pitted his wits and his energies are barely remembered and rarely celebrated, whereas the work of Christian charity is often the first and last presence among the needy.

In an article published in 1999 entitled 'How Liberalism fails the Church' Cardinal George of Chicago wrote in praise of Newman, Ozanam and other nineteenth-century Catholics observing that 'While they differed profoundly in their analyses and their conclusions, common to each one's thinking was a rejection of certain cultural aspects of modernity, particularly materialism, secularism, moral relativism, and individualism. Also common to each was the conviction that only a unified, energetic, convincing, and engaged church could solve these developing cultural problems.' It is interesting to note that while Mill would have dissented from the recommended cure he shared something of this diagnosis of the cultural ills of his own age. That common diagnosis is a legacy that may continue to be drawn on today, meriting in Hume's words 'the durable admiration which attends those works that have survived all the caprices of mode and fashion'.

Section III
Faith and reason

11.

Philosophy in the life of the Church

The Second Vatican Council was conceived in part out of a concern to open the Church to the wider world in order that the former might better dispose itself for the benefit of the latter. Ideally nothing good would be lost from the Church, and the process of development might be advanced so as to bring forth abundant and appealing blossoms followed by further wholesome fruit.

Notwithstanding the strident complaints from different quarters that the Council failed in its aims, either by leaving the Church an inward-looking and defensive bastion of anti-modernists, or by fostering doctrinal dissent, moral relativism and liturgical barbarism, the fact is that at this distance, and amidst the other changes of the second half of the twentieth century, it remains hard to judge the general effect of the Council. It may also be a mistake to suppose that even positive development in the life of the Church can be a process of gain without loss.

One might reply that loss will not matter if the net result is gain, i.e. more good; but apart from the risk of sliding into theological consequentialism there is also the possibility, emphasised in secular terms by some philosophers, that any field of values is comprised of a plurality of genuine but incommensurable goods, such that the pursuit of any one may of necessity be at the expense of another. Socialists and libertarians have often sought to define liberty and equality in ways that eliminate the appearance of tensions between these values. Thus egalitarians have often held that the redistribution of resources is liberty promoting; while libertarians have maintained that economic freedom expresses the equal right of all to the ownership of their labour and its fruits. We are now unlikely to regard these claims as anything but self-serving sophistries, for we can see that the redistribution of wealth involves non-voluntary transfers, and freedom can easily be at the cost of distributive justice. The implication is not that if we choose to pursue one policy the other turns out not to have value, but rather that, whichever we choose, to some extent at least, we lose something genuinely worth having.

Similarly, whatever the real value of the following policies, a greater emphasis on transparency and intelligibility in liturgy is liable to be at the cost of the sense of transcendence and profundity; the promotion of pastoral study and of social justice ethics is likely to diminish understanding of fundamental moral theology and to dilute the sense of personal sin; the cultivation of the notion of a 'pilgrim Church' travelling towards a destination it has not reached and which may remain far off makes problematic the idea of the ark of salvation furnished with the deposit of faith. I am not concerned to debate what in these cases counts as gain and what loss, but only to point out what change involves and to suggest that it is in no one's interest to pretend otherwise. Whether, overall, the post-Vatican Church is better or worse than that which preceded it is a question that should be felt to be difficult to answer, and even problematic to contemplate, for it is after all one and the same Church as was founded by Christ and as will persist until his return.

This said, one can certainly look at particular ways in which the Church and Catholic life and culture more generally differ now from the pre-Vatican period and consider what gains and losses the changes have involved. I wish to do something of this with regard to philosophy, relating the history of the practice within Catholic circles to that in the English-speaking world more generally. The restriction to the English-speaking world is for reasons of space and circumstance, but given the extent and influence of British and American philosophy this is hardly a parochial restriction. As well as describing the past and characterising the present I aim to say something about the future as it might be, and, as I believe, it should be.

Anyone raised in or otherwise familiar with the Roman Catholic tradition will recognise at least something of the extent to which it has long drawn upon philosophy to shape and defend its teachings. Yet even if it was inevitable that this should happen, it was certainly not obvious to members of the Early Church that Jerusalem had much to do with Athens. In anticipation of his journey to the heart of the Roman Empire St Paul appealed to rational reflection, maintaining that 'What can be known about God is perfectly plain for men to see, for God has shown it to them: ever since the creation of the world, the invisible existence of God and his everlasting power have been clearly seen by the mind's understanding of created things' (Romans 1:19–20, 57–8). Given that his intended readership was probably largely one of educated Gentile Romans it is perhaps unsurprising to find him writing in terms reminscent of Cicero's observation in the widely read philosophical work *On the Nature of the Gods* that 'nothing can be so obvious and clear, as we gaze up at the sky and observe the heavenly bodies, as that there is some divine power of surpassing intelligence by which they are ordered' (Bk. II).

Yet the unhappiness of Paul's own direct engagement with the sages of Athens must have been fresh in his mind: Acts tells us that when he spoke to the philosophers 'at his mention of rising from the dead, some of them burst out laughing' and around the same time he quoted with approval from Isaiah where it is written that the wisdom of the wise is doomed (Isaiah 29:14;), adding on his own account that 'God chose those who by human standards are fools to shame the wise … what I spoke and proclaimed was not meant to convince by philosophical argument but to demonstrate the convincing power of the Spirit' (1 Corinthians 1:27; 2:4).

If there is a tension here it is easy enough to see how it might be resolved. According to Paul, reason is able to discern general truths about the existence of a Deity and his governance of the world – hence there is no excuse for ungodliness; but it is foolish to think that human wisdom is adequate to discern the nature of God or that the unaided will is sufficient to bring men to salvation – hence the need of revelation and of grace. This combination is a coherent one and it later took the form of a distinction between the preambles to faith and the dogmatic content of the faith itself, *depositum fidei*. Viewed from the perspective of rational enquiry it is reasonable to read Paul's passage in Romans as an instance, be it a limited one, of natural theology, and hence as an implicit endorsement of philosophy of religion so conceived. What it remains silent on, however, is the validity and value of the practice that has come to be known as philosophical theology. The latter makes no distinction between the sources of the concepts and propositions it investigates (natural or revealed), but is concerned to evaluate them in terms of their coherence, intelligibility and possible truth.

It is not difficult to construct a Pauline case against philosophical theology on the grounds that if the concepts investigated are other than those delivered by natural theology or by Christian revelation then it is at best idle and at worst blasphemous; if they are of the latter sorts then the Gospel tells one all one needs to know. Yet apart from the fact that there might be some intellectual value in investigating ideas to which one is not antecedently committed, the fact is that there is a real question of how to understand Gospel teachings. Moreover, as the Church developed so its theology broadened and deepened, and ideas were generated of which Paul could have had little understanding, even where they derived from things he himself had introduced such as that Christ's resurrection instituted a new creation (1 Corinthians), that believers are one body in Christ (Romans), and that righteousness is to be associated with faith not works (Galatians).

Accordingly, rational reflection upon Christian ideas seems not merely legitimate but required.

That conclusion was reached long ago, implicitly at least by the time of the First Council of Nicea (325) at which the *homoousion* ('of one substance') formulation was received as orthodox in preference to *homoiousion* ('of like substance'), and by the Middle Ages theologians moved with ease between general reasoning about the existence and nature of God and specific argumentation concerning the Trinity, the Incarnation, the Communion of Saints, and the varieties and operations of Grace. Modern readers of Aquinas are liable to be impressed by his range, which is indeed astonishing, but they would do well to attend to the fact that this crosses all sorts of regions between which later writers, particularly in the Protestant tradition, such as Kierkegaard and Barth, attempted to erect barriers. Since for Barth reason is unable to achieve knowledge of God which is available only through the divine revelation in Jesus Christ, it follows that natural theology is an impossibility – as is substantive dialogue with non-Christians.

While the medievals of the Latin Church did not exactly practice inter-faith dialogue they were certainly willing to learn from Jewish and Muslim philosopher-theologians such as Maimonides (Moses ben Maimon) and Avicenna (Ibn-Sina), referring to them with respect; and although the Reformation put Catholicism on the defensive it did not curb the practice of interweaving philosophy and theology. It is true that scholasticism declined in the seventeenth and eighteenth centuries but that was due to the general Western rejection of Aristotelianism upon which medieval Christian/philosophical syntheses had drawn. Aquinas was named a Doctor of the Church in 1568, five years after the close of the Council of Trent and seven after the birth of Francis Bacon. The next forty years would see the births of Hobbes and Descartes, and within a century Aristotelianism had been widely rejected in favour of empiricist and rationalist philosophies that regarded Catholic theology as being either insufficiently warranted by history and experience or else too closely tied to them.

The fate of scholasticism reflected the general circumstance of the Church in the modern period: battered from without and subject to conflict within. The intellectual and social disruptions of the eighteenth and nineteenth centuries unsettled Catholic education and scholarship and resulted in a confused plurality of opinions and approaches. In part because of this some church leaders saw a need to re-establish a coherent position. In 1846 the newly elected Pius IX reaffirmed the compatibility of faith and reason and in so doing encouraged a return to scholasticism. Explicit papal endorsement of the medieval style of synthesis, and more precisely of that provided by Aquinas, came in 1879 with the encyclical *Aeterni Patris* published by Leo XIII in the year following his own election as succesor to Pius. The Thomist revival quickly took root in Continental Europe, initially among religious but later among lay intellectuals, and from there it was exported to Britain and more importantly to the United States.

Angelo Giuseppe Roncalli was born two years after the publication of *Aeterni Patris*. Within a year of becoming Pope John XXIII in 1958 he too had an announcement to make to the universal Church, namely that he wished to convene an Oecumenical Council for the purpose of renewing its religious life and re-expressing the substance of its faith. At that time most Catholics engaged in philosophy were Thomists. Much of what they thought, talked and wrote about was internal to the scholastic tradition being concerned with the interpretation of Aquinas's texts and doctrines, and with debating the merits of later interpretations and developments. While a few looked outward in order to engage with other traditions, the vast majority regarded modern non-scholastic philosophy as a series of errors to be avoided or refuted. Pius XII's 1950 encyclical *Humani Generis* condemned a range of positions that were gaining ground in post-war theology (including some dissent from seminary scholasticism). An adaptation of the phrase used as the English title of the encyclical could well serve to characterise the view of empiricism, rationalism and idealism held by most mid-century Thomists , viz. 'false trends in modern thought'.

It is hard to say exactly when the change came but it began in Europe and North America with a series of studies of post-Kantian continental philosophers: Hegel, Marx, Kierkegaard, Husserl, Heidegger and Sartre, and progresses towards appropriation and not just description of their views. By the close of Vatican II in 1965 the pre-eminence of Thomism was seriously threatened and by the end of the following decade it was but one strand of Catholic philosophical thought and a diminishing one at that. Significantly, however, intellectual *aggiornamento* tended not to draw upon the form of philosophy dominant within the English-speaking world, namely conceptual analysis.

There are two main reasons for this. First, the very idea of clarifying the content of terms can seem a trivialisation of philosophical enquiry and not at all suited to the presentation of transcendental subject matter – it was common even within Britain to complain that this style of philosophy was just concerned with 'words'. Second, it was generally assumed that the sort of philosophy that was practised in Oxford and Cambridge and in Harvard and Berkeley was essentially 'logical positivism' which was famously associated with the claim of A. J. Ayer and others that religious, moral and aesthetic statements are meaningless. This second consideration also encouraged the turn to 'continental' thought among Catholics disenchanted or just bored with Thomism. It was well known that most continental and analytic thinkers had mutual disdain for one another's philosophies; and since analytic thought was presumed to be hostile to religion many Catholics inferred that an enemy of that approach must be a friend.

My own view is that overall these trends have been unfortunate, for while there is no doubt that the seminary scholasticism of the 1950s was often a dull and degenerate form of what in its medieval heyday was a glorious tradition, it was a serious mistake to abandon Thomism given its claim to be the most effective general synthesis of Catholic doctrine and philosophical truth, thus far achieved. In addition, it is a mistake to suppose that analytical philosophy – the philosophy of Russell, G. E. Moore, the early and later Wittgenstein, Elizabeth Anscombe, Peter Geach, Donald Davidson, Michael Dummett, Bernard Williams, Hilary Putnam, and Saul Kripke and of many others – is simply concerned with clarifying concepts or that it is the continuation of logical positivism by other means. Of the philosophers listed half are theists and three are Roman Catholics: Anscombe, Geach and Dummett. All of those named have contributed significantly to the pursuit of deep and important issues concerning the nature of reality and character of human thought and action; and the Catholics have all addressed topics of enduring religious interest such as proofs of the existence of God and the nature of God's operations in the world. Furthermore, the turn to continental thought, particularly in its recent post-modernist variants, far from bolstering the claims of the faith has tended to produce in those who have taken that route a kind of ironic agnosticism, and even a convoluted and unspoken atheism.

More to the point, however, is the fact that philosophers in the English-speaking world are now increasingly open to different styles of enquiry and to the full history of the subject to a far greater extent than has ever been the case. In this respect at least the present is a rich and promising age. Where British, American and Australasian thinkers stand in greatest need of development is in respect of what John Paul II describes in *Fides et Ratio* as the 'sapiential dimension' of philosophy. There he writes of a crisis of meaning arising from a fragmentation of knowledge consequent upon scientific development, and from an aura of scepticism produced by the proliferation of philosophical and related theories of the world and human life (§81). It is well worth quoting in full what John Paul has to say on the matter of how philosophy might now proceed:

> To be consonant with the word of God, philosophy needs first of all to recover its sapiential dimension as a search for the ultimate and overlapping meaning of life. This first requirement is in fact most helpful in stimulating philosophy to conform to its proper nature. In doing so, it will be not only the decisive factor which determines the foundations and limits of the different fields of scientific learning, but will also take its place as the ultimate framework of the unity of human knowledge and action, leading them to converge towards a final goal and meaning. This sapiential dimension is all the more necessary today, because the immense expansion of humanity's technical capability demands a renewed and sharpened sense of ultimate values. *Faith and Reason*, 1998, pp. 119–20

John XXIII attributed his calling of Vatican II to the inspiration of the Holy Spirit. Whatever its source, the intention of opening the Church to the wider world in order that that which was established by Christ might more effectively serve all humanity was a noble one. It is superficially ironic that in the period since the Council the influence of the Church in the world appears to have declined. Some, of course, argue that the former was the cause of the latter, but anyone familiar with the general trend of Western culture over the last three centuries will know that the decline began long before the Council, so that the critics are not even in the position of having committed the fallacy *post hoc ergo propter hoc*. The current position of religion in Europe is in part a consequence of the philosophically sceptical temper of modernity and in part a result of a rampant combination of individualism, materialism and hedonism. These causes have given rise to a variety of worrying trends: to the substitution of technology for learning, to the growth of relativism, to the commodification of relationships, to

the decline of marriage and the family, and to the instru-
mentalisation of life itself. In the world of politics we have
become familiar with the management of effects, but what
science and philosophy both teach is that conditions are
cured not by treating the symptoms but by tackling the
causes.

Philosophy is sometimes castigated for its practical
irrelevance. Yet nothing could be more relevant than a
means of changing minds, for while natural forces may
reconfigure the face of the earth, it is minds – and only
minds – that can change the world in accord with a plan
and a set of values. John XXIII saw the necessity for the
Church to re-express the substance of the faith in terms
intelligible to the contemporary world, and John Paul II
has seen the need to have a clear and effective understanding of the nature of philosophy in order to use it to
think about matters of substance.

Neither perception diminishes the achievements of the
past but both require Catholic philosophers to think hard
about how best to carry the subject forward so as to be true
to its vocation as the love of wisdom and to be effective in
engaging the problems that confront us. There are those
who will say that all would have been well if we had held
fast to the Thomism that prevailed in Catholic circles in
the first half of the twentieth century; and there are those
who would consign that tradition to the wasteland of failed
metaphysical approaches. Neither judgement is sound and
both exhibit the tendency to think that all change must
either be deterioration or improvement. As I remarked in
the opening section, change necessarily occasions loss, but
just as one should not regard this as implying a worsening
simpliciter nor should one think that if something
good comes to be that this shows that overall change is for
the best.

The primary task facing philosophers today is that of
giving substance and general purpose to their enquiries.
In so far as philosophy is an intellectual discipline it needs
to be rigorous and precise (to the extent that any particu-

lar subject matter allows). Analytical philosophy has made virtues of rigour and precision, and since its rediscovery of metaphysics some forty years ago it is more likely to put these virtues to significant use. At the same time it tends not to have a reflective sense of its own nature as an activity directed towards comprehensive truth. By contrast, continental European philosophy in the styles best known to the layperson, speaks grandly of the totality while failing to deliver much in the way of rigorous and precise argumentation. Readers of the *Summa Theologiae* and of Aquinas's 'disputed questions', and of his commentaries on works of Aristotle will know that he manages to maintain a sense of the structure and importance of the wood, while also identifying the distinguishing features of, and navigating between, the trees. That provides an excellent model, but if the substance of Aquinas's Catholic/Aristotelian synthesis is to be communicated and win converts it must first be cast in a form intelligible to the best and most rigorous non-Catholic thinkers of the day. To achieve this it would be wise to consider the forms deployed by those very thinkers, not in the spirit of uncritical emulation but in that of further synthesis. Happily this has been happening for some while and there is evidence, confirmed by the increasing use of the expression 'analytical thomism' that the efforts at constructive engagement are bearing fruit.

Yet the task of philosophical *aggiornamento* is not complete, and in the nature of the case it never can be short of the end of the world and the final coming of the Kingdom. That may well be some way off; on the other hand it is an old and good practice to prepare for it as if it may happen at any time. Philosophers who took the latter possibility seriously might well attach priority to developing the sapiential dimension of the subject, which is perhaps one reason why John Paul II recommends attention to it.

G. K. Chesterton once observed that philosophy is just thought that has been thought out. More strictly one might say that it is thought-out thought about the highest things as these admit of rational contemplation. That kind of thinking has to have a central place within the life of the Church and of the world; otherwise human beings will have failed to realise their nature as rational creatures made in the image of God for the purpose of knowing, loving and serving Him. There really is no merit in looking back to a supposed golden age of pre-Vatican II Catholicism, for even if some things were better then than now others were worse, and in any case the Catholic should live facing forwards – the direction of life itself.

12.

Religion, philosophy and faith

The existence of God, the meaning of life, and the possibility of life after death all engage the imagination and the intellect. As a philosopher I spend my time assessing the coherence and cogency of ideas and arguments; but reason has its limits, and some matters seem resistant to conclusive proof. Religion may be one of these.

Of course, there is no such thing as 'religion' any more than there is such a creature as an 'animal'. Every religion has its distinguishing myths and scriptures, its dogmas and doctrines; and every faith has its denominations and sects. Amazingly, there are over 20,000 different Christian denominations, and over 9,000 distinct and separate religions, with a 100 or so new ones coming into being every year.

In the West we are most familiar with a range of faiths (Judaism, Christianity and Islam) that share a belief in a single, all-knowing, all-good, all-powerful, eternal God who created and sustains the universe. Ironically, however, it is principally within societies which once subscribed to this 'theistic' vision that it is claimed that religion is irrelevant. Why should that be?

Believers cite affluence as distracting us from the things that really matter: *God, the soul, and eternity*; while atheists also point to material development – but as freeing us from such superstitions. Yet, if people no longer attend the synagogues, churches, and mosques of their parents and grandparents, why do they persist in believing in the 'spiritual', turning to prayer in times of need, and hoping for life beyond the grave? For there is little reason to believe in, practice and hope for these save on the basis of a traditional faith.

The opponents of religion are liable to view these beliefs as remnants of former faith, and to point instead to opinion polls showing decline in religious attendance as evidence for a deeper loss of belief. But the relationship between such surveys and claims of religious decline is arguably the reverse of what is usually claimed. Rather than polls grounding a scientific assessment, the secularist thought has tended to be father to the sociological deed. Over the course of a century or so, the view has developed that religion has been subverted by natural science, and that religious practice has been exposed as self-deception or social manipulation. In consequence, many secularists presume that traditional religion must be in decline *because it ought to be*, and so fashion and interpret surveys accordingly.

An example, typical of the confident secularism of its period, is Peter Berger's statement in an interview with the *New York Times* at the end of the 1960s; that 'by the twenty-first century religious believers are likely to be found only in small sects, huddled together to resist a world-wide secular culture'. In retrospect this prediction simply looks absurd. Over one third of the world's population (almost two billion people) are Christians, and half of this number are Roman Catholics. Islam also has in excess of a billion adherents and it is set to become Europe's and America's second religion. In the twenty-first century it is atheists that are huddled together to resist a world-wide religious culture.

Yet there is one indisputable truth in the secularist thesis: namely that in western societies, and increasingly in other parts of the world to which those societies have exported their popular culture, there is growing ignorance of things religious. For secular humanists and scientific atheists that is as it should be. For committed believers it is a matter for profound sadness. Whose attitude is the right one cannot be discovered by consulting polls, but only by considering the coherence, plausibility and truth of fundamental religious claims. The most important question that a reflective person can pursue in considering the issue of religion is not *do* people believe it? but *should* they?

It is a fact little appreciated, even by quite orthodox believers, that the Roman Catholic Church holds as a matter of dogma that the existence of God can be established by the 'natural light of reason'. As the text of Vatican I puts it, 'let him [who denies it] be anathema'. This was a bold declaration in the nineteenth century; at the end of the twentieth it would seem to some to be self-evident folly. Quite apart from atheists who suppose that reason establishes the non-existence of God, there is a widely held opinion that the existence of God is a prime example of the sort of thing that cannot be demonstrated *one way or the other*.

Let me begin with the latter position. One argument for it is that, by definition, the idea of God is that of an entity transcendent of human categories of thought, a 'super-something we know not what'. But something of which we can say nothing cannot be comprehended let alone made the subject of an existence proof – or, indeed, of a non-existence proof. At best we might say there *may* be a 'something' beyond the things of which we have knowledge; but the character of those things cannot be drawn upon to describe this something or to give reason to believe that it exists. Accordingly, the rational position is one of silent agnosticism.

This is emotionally frustrating but it is also philosophically naive. Much of fundamental science deals in unobserved and, in principle unobservable, entities – things too small, too distant or too strange to observe – yet reference to them is an essential part of well-supported scientific theories. What gives those theories credibility is their explanatory power. Likewise, according to the theist

philosopher, we are justified in believing in the existence
of God because such a being serves to explain – in a way
that nothing else can – the existence and the nature of the
world.

First, then, its existence: Thomas Aquinas presents a
clear and succinct account of the main theistic proofs (the
famous 'five ways') in his *Summa Theologiae* (Ia, q2.)
Interestingly, in the first three of these proofs he himself
argues to a kind of 'believing agnosticism'. His claim is
that if anything comes into being or changes, then ultimately there must be a something which neither comes to
be, nor changes, nor passes away, but which is the first
cause of existence and change in other things. I call this
stance 'believing agnosticism' because the conclusion of
the arguments is just that there is a transcendent source of
the world – no more, and no less, than this.

Of course, Aquinas thought that we are in fact entitled
to say a great deal more about God, but that most of what
we know comes from revelation and not from pure reason.
This said, his fifth proof, which concerns the appearance
of order in the world, starts to put 'flesh' on the bones of
the very abstract *cause-of-being-and-change*. A purposeful, intelligent and benign form begins to emerge from
considering the regular and productive activity of organisms and other parts of nature. The appearance of design
in the functioning of the organs of animals and in their
overall behaviour is not naturally explicable and hence if it
is to be explained at all then its source must lie beyond
nature.

Following Darwin, it is standardly objected that the
appearance of directed activity is actually explicable in
entirely natural terms. Chance mutation gives rise to
features that are advantageous to their possessors; beings
so advantaged have a greater chance of survival and so
breed more extensively; and by repetition of this combination of mutation and adaptation complex animals have
evolved. Contemporary biblical creationists argue against
Darwinian-style evolutionary naturalism by citing the

absence of an adequate fossil record of the supposed multitude of intermediary species between worms and higher animals. This is not a very plausible response. For one thing the conditions of fossilisation are not uniformly present; for another the evidence of species development is very good. I believe, however, that this rejoinder is not the end of the design argument, and that a good case can be made to show that no wholly natural explanation of the emergence of life, of species development, and, in particular, of the appearance of *Homo Sapiens* can be given.

To take just the last of these, human beings have powers of thought that seem entirely distinct from physical processes. Material interactions are always between individual objects: one cat fights with another, one ember ignites a piece of paper, and so on. In thought, however, we enter an order of general features and of non-existent entities. I can think of catness or of heat as such (though there are no such things in nature) and I can contemplate might-have-been and never-to-be scenarios. These powers of universal and abstract thought are deeply mysterious yet definitive of human beings. If they are physicalistically inexplicable then there cannot be a naturalistic account of their emergence, and if naturalism fails then either there is no explanation or there is a non-natural one. Thus we are returned to Aquinas's argument for design.

Since some readers will find this approach somewhat abstract and spiritually unappealing let me offer a more 'soul-grasping' case. In his great work the *Confessions* (c.397), St Augustine charts his own journey to Christianity, and writes of the fallen condition of human beings as involving 'the darkening of the intellect and the disturbance of the passions'. Are these not all-too evident throughout the world? For Augustine there is something further to be discovered in our lives: a pattern of beginning, rising and falling, not imposed from without, but originating in our free choices. The same pattern can be seen in the affairs of nations and empires. We can see it daily in ourselves as we set out to act well in pursuit of higher values, and then fall back into baseness.

The fact of this pattern can hardly be denied. What is at issue is its significance. The atheist may look for an explanation in genetics, evolution, economics, or food additives; but none of these really seems to capture the sense that it points to a transcendent destiny. Religion offers an explanation and a solution. In the words of Augustine:

> Man being part of your creation desires to praise you – man who carries with him his mortality, the witness of his sin ... for you have formed us for yourself; and our hearts are restless until they find their rest in you.

Human beings were made by God in order to share in his life, rather as human parents have children not for benefit but to share their lives with. What we crave is absolute, unconditional, and everlasting *love*, and that is precisely what theism offers through the idea of an afterlife spent in the company of God. If that hope is illusory then we are the most miserable of animals, and no talk of 'Enlightenment' or of 'human progress' can begin to provide an adequate alternative. It is, I think, God or nothing – and only a *real* God will do.

Philosophical theism is intellectually credible but it is not the stuff of faith. That, however, is not an argument against it but only a reminder of the fact that Christian belief draws extensively on revealed truth for its content, and draws wholly upon the supernatural gift of grace for its identity as *faith* and not opinion. Both faithless reason and unreasonable faith are conditions apt for improvement.

13.

Who's afraid of evolution?

Reflecting on the recent and ongoing furore about creationism, evolution, and intelligent design is a depressing business, for the whole thing has become hideously confused: an untidy tangle of science, philosophy, theology, politics and culture. Recently the Archbishop of Canterbury entered the debate by saying that creationism should not be taught in the classroom, as is reportedly already happening in some city academies and other schools. Interviewed by the *Guardian* he is quoted as saying

> I think creationism is a kind of category mistake, as if the bible were a theory like other theories ... It's not as if the writer of Genesis or whatever sat down and said well, how am I going to explain all this ... I know 'In the beginning God created the heavens and the earth'. I don't think [creationism] should be taught, actually. And that's different from saying ... discussing, teaching about what creation means. For that matter, it's not even the same as saying that Darwinism is the only thing that ought to be taught. My worry is creationism can end up reducing the doctrine of creation, rather than enhancing it.

Rowan Williams is a scholar familiar with the development of Christian doctrine and wants to avoid crude reductions to simple formulae, but his quoted words may leave some readers wondering what the doctrine of creation is, if not creationism. Before addressing that, let me explain something of the blast and noise emanating from America over the issue of evolution and intelligent design.

This is sometimes described as being about the nature of science, and the limits of credible belief, but more than anything it is an aspect of an ongoing culture war between progressive secular liberals and traditional religious conservatives. The former have an agenda for change covering a whole range of educational, moral and social issues, while the latter have an agenda for resistance or restoration in just the same areas. The immediate battle-ground of these oppositions shifts: sometimes it is marriage and family; sometimes it is education and lifestyles. Below these slippery surfaces, however, lies the solid base of belief about the nature of human kind and its place in the universe.

Recently it has suited both sides to fight over evolution and creation, but in doing so there has been a confusion, often intentional, of scientific, theological and philosophical ideas. At its crudest, *biblical creationism* is the claim that the universe came into being a few thousand years in more or less the form in which we see it now. That is clearly incompatible with more or less universally held scientific beliefs about the age of the universe, the origins of the earth and the development of life upon it. If there is a place for telling children about *biblical creationism* it may be in history or social studies but not in science.

At its simplest, *cosmological naturalism* means that the origins of the universe, the world and of all life within it, past and present, are wholly explicable in terms of physical processes including those of random mutation and natural selection through environmental fitness. This is incompatible not only with *biblical creationism* but with less extravagant religious positions such as that the universe was created and that human beings have a special spiritual nature.

That it has these further implications reveals that *cosmological naturalism* is more than a scientific claim, it is a philosophical one, since the evidence of the evolution of species, say, is independent of the issue of the origins of the universe or the question whether human beings have non-material aspects. These latter issues of cosmic origin and human nature are not empirical in the usual understanding, but belong to metaphysics. The scientific evidence will not decide between them. By symmetry, therefore *cosmological naturalism* is not a proper subject for science classes but might usefully be discussed in philosophy or religious studies.

What then of *neo-Darwinianism* on the one hand, and of '*Intelligent Design*' on the other? Well, as the philosopher C. E. M. Joad was apt to say, 'it depends what you mean by . . .'. If *neo-Darwinianism* is the claim that there is an ancient evolutionary history by which species have emerged from one another through processes of variation and natural selection, then it is a scientific hypothesis for which there is overwhelming evidence and it would be irresponsible to teach biology at school without introducing and explaining this as a powerful scientific explanation. If on the other hand it is code for *cosmological naturalism* then its claims have transcended science and belong in philosophical discussions.

Likewise if *intelligent design* is a rival hypothesis about the causes of specific biological structures and processes, claiming that they show evidence of having been designed, it has some claim to be explored in science but it is unlikely to fare well against the non-design alternative. If, however, it is code for *biblical creationism* then again it has no place in science and most theologically sophisticated teachers would feel it deserved little attention even in a religion class.

Finally, what ought to be the religious believer's attitude to evolutionary theory? 'It depends what you mean by . . .'; but, that said, a traditional Jew, Christian or Muslim must remain committed to three ideas:

1. that the universe is the product of creation;

2. that the course of the universe is under the providential governance of God; and
3. that human beings are images of God in the respect of having a spiritual (non-material) aspect to their nature.

Those three ideas are each incompatible with *cosmological naturalism*, though not with evolution by natural selection, and in one sense they constitute a very definite kind of creationism – but not the wild kind.

I began by referring to the furore surrounding these issues and this, of course, has been the subject of much media coverage. Rowan Williams's comments came in the course of a newspaper interview. Indeed it is interesting to note in an age of apparent unbelief, secular newspapers and magazines continue to devote so much attention to religion. Admittedly, this is not in a spirit of invoking religious teachings as a source of knowledge about reality and human nature, or as a guide to personal life or to the formulating of social policies. Also, articles offering spiritual reflections are now few. Yet the press continues to report debates within the Christian Churches, and to relate pronouncements by their leaders.

Any element of controversy (such as the Archbishop of Canterbury's more recent comments about accommodating Sharia law), encourages such stories; but a more significant reason for continuing religious reporting is because journalists know that, notwithstanding decline in church attendance and in general knowledge of religious ideas and teachings, we remain interested in the nature of the cosmos, in the origin of human beings, and in the meaning of life; these three are all the business of religion, if not its sole preserve.

So it was that more recently the press contained articles reporting and commenting on Pope Benedict's observation that evolutionary theory has not been confirmed. Some editors believed there was a story to be got from a seeming disagreement between his remarks and the words of Pope John Paul II from 1996, when he said that evolution is 'more than a hypothesis', interpreted as meaning that it is an established fact.

Pope Benedict referred to this, writing 'My predecessor had his reasons for saying this, but it is also true that the theory of evolution is not a complete, scientifically proven theory', adding that it is 'not finally provable [because] we cannot haul 10,000 generations into the laboratory'.

Clearly these are important matters concerning nothing less than the truth about our origins and our fundamental nature. Christian belief holds that we are part of a created order which expresses the supreme intelligence and providential care of God, and that we are in part spiritual beings created for a supernatural destiny. Evolution appears to be in conflict with these ideas; and now we seem to be in confusion with successive Pontiffs speaking at odds about the status of evolutionary theory. Some explanation is called for.

Before providing it let me quote further from John Paul's 1996 remarks, and from the observations of Pope Benedict in a newly published book entitled *Creation and Evolution* containing the proceedings of a private seminar held at Castel Gandolfo in September 2006.

First John Paul:

There is no conflict between evolution and the doctrine of the faith. In order to mark out the limits of their own proper fields theologians and those working on the exegesis of the Scripture need to be well-informed regarding the results of the latest scientific research.

Next, Benedict:

The question is not to either make a decision for a creationism that excludes science, or for an evolutionary theory that covers its own gaps and does not want to see the questions that reach beyond the methodological possibilities of natural science. The theory of evolution implies that questions must be assigned to philosophy and which themselves lead beyond the realms of science.

Apparently, then, we find John Paul holding that there is no conflict between evolutionary theory and Christian doctrine, and even accepting the former as now established, and his successor maintaining that the theory remains unproven and is in any case an inadequate explanation of human origins. Disagreement at such a level in the Church on such a fundamental issue would be striking indeed and properly troubling for Catholics.

In fact, however, there is no significant opposition and the two sets of comments are compatible, though there is a difference in emphasis and purpose. To see how this is so and to address the broader issues of evolution and creation it is necessary to distinguish between '*Evolution*' and '*Evolutionism*'.

The first is an empirical theory of the development and differentiation of animal species. The most prominent version of this theory is *neo-Darwinianism* as described above in its guise as a scientific hypothesis. Evolutionism, by contrast, is a comprehensive and partly metaphysical theory of the origins and nature of all terrestrial life, including the emergence and character of homo sapiens. Thus it is a version of *cosmological naturalism*.

Evolution holds that the range of species existing today and in the past is the result of variation in reproduction and of natural selection on the basis of organisms' fittedness to their environments. Variety in the characteristics of 'offspring' means that some are better, and others worse, adapted to the world. The better fitted are more likely to live long enough to reproduce, and so their kind survives. Over generations, however, new characteristics emerge and so the process of diversification and consolidation continues, resulting in the rich variety of species alive today, including human kind.

Evolution so described is a theory or hypothesis designed to explain existing life forms, the fossil record, and the apparent relations between these. Like any theory it is open to challenge, and since most species are irrecoverably lost in the past the claim that they developed from one another through a common lineage is not directly confirmable. As Benedict said 'we can't haul 10,000 generations into the laboratory'.

This said, there can be no serious doubt that

1. the history of life on earth is very ancient;
2. there has been species-development, with later forms emerging out of earlier ones; and
3. the lineage of human beings connects them with other parts of the family of terrestrial life.

Evolutionism, however, goes further, insisting that

4. the emergence of life out of inanimate matter,
5. the development of consciousness, and
6. the appearance of thinking, deliberating beings, are all the products of a purely physical process leading to chance variations in replication.

This not only goes beyond the empirical evidence but includes claims, in particular about all processes being physical, and the course of biological evolution being due to chance, that could not be empirically confirmed since they are really philosophical theses presented under the guise of scientific ones.

Catholics should not be intimidated by the assertion that 'science has shown' that we are products of blind chance and entirely physical causes; but they should also set out to challenge it, and expose its own difficulties. One such is that of explaining consciousness, thought and moral action as involving nothing other than material processes. Another is that of accounting for the natural causal regularities that govern the operations of matter itself.

Perhaps with a concern about biblical fundamentalism giving religion a bad name, and with a genuine regard for the achievements of science as also expressing the gifts of thought and intelligence, Pope John Paul was pleased to acknowledge that *Evolution* had established itself as more than a mere hypothesis. That, however, does nothing to prove *Evolutionism,* and given the increasing drift towards the latter, perhaps Pope Benedict has judged that it is time to take up the challenge of refuting it, not with 'creation science' but with philosophical argument.

We need now to try to prove what we already believe, that the natural world is the product not of chance physical processes but of purposeful reason – in short, of *logos.*

14.

The Church cannot do without intellectuals

The notion of 'ideas' as it features in contemporary politics is increasingly that of the advertising agent. In this understanding an idea is not so much a unit of intellectual thought as a marketing concept, or the mental equivalent of a catch phrase: something to be remembered rather than explored: 'think small', 'let your fingers do the walking', 'reach out and touch someone', and 'sometimes you feel like a nut, and sometimes you don't'.

This way of thinking about ideas is now very familiar, but it is quite unlike that which prevailed in the half-century between the General Strike of 1926 and the beginning of the Thatcher revolution in 1979. During that period the political order was divided along philosophical grounds, with notions of individual, community, state, democracy, authority, freedom, and justice, finely honed and skilfully deployed by advocates of one or another political theory. In such an environment anyone who carelessly talked in clichés risked being brought to a rapid halt with the demand 'What do you mean – exactly?'.

People who were then serious about ideas also recognised that they tend to group together into systems, of which theories and ideologies are but the most familiar examples. So, to enter the world of ideas was to become a traveller through intellectual space, charting a course from one conceptual cluster to the next. And to do that required skill and training: one needed to have been taught how to think, and preferably to have studied the thinking of greater minds.

It is little surprise, perhaps, that a period of serious political thought was also one of serious philosophical and religious thinking. Indeed they were often linked. In his (1942) review of T. S. Eliot's *The Dry Salvages*, Orwell remarked that 'Sooner or later one is obliged to adopt a positive stance towards life and society. It would be putting it too crudely to say that every poet in our time must either die young, enter the Catholic Church, or join the Communist Party, but in fact the escape from the consciousness of futility is along these general lines.'

Orwell himself managed to avoid both Catholicism and Communism, but he shared with members of those faiths a sense that for human beings life is, or should be, a mental and moral challenge; something to be understood and lived accordingly, rather than gone through like an extended piece of popular entertainment. That, and the education he received and the training he subjected himself to, made him an intellectual.

In his day, as in ours, there were many atheist thinkers; but then there were also many intellectual believers. Indeed, there was a widespread sense that a Christian who had the ability, thereby also had the obligation to think seriously about theological, moral and even philosophical ideas, in ways that would not only deepen his or her understanding but enable him or her to engage in serious conversation with enemies of belief, as well as with the doubtful and the know-not-whats.

The need for Catholic intellectuals is no less now than it was in the twentieth century. Indeed it is greater. People like Orwell, and leading thinkers in the generations preceding and succeeding his, may have rejected Catholicism; but they also respected it as something deserving of intellectual scrutiny. They perceived it as being at once a faith, a system of thought, and a patron and vehicle of high culture; as well as a source of spiritual aid and counsel.

Writing in 1959 in *The Riddle of Roman Catholicism*,

the Lutheran theologian Jaroslav Pelikan, observed that 'The road to Rome has often been the road to a synthesis of faith and intellect which appeared impossible anywhere else.' That road has not closed, but it is increasingly less well known, having become obscured by falls and under-growth, and no longer being so well maintained or sign-posted.

By the end of the First World War the old sense of the world as being under the governance of a good and caring God had been torn and blasted. Yet it was just then that the Catholic Evidence Guild was founded in the Westminster diocese with the purpose of enabling clergy and lay speakers 'to make known the Catholic Faith'. It soon spread: by 1925 there were one hundred and twenty speakers, holding forty meetings a week. Fifty years before the Guild was established, Herbert (later Cardinal) Vaughan had founded the Catholic Truth Society, later re-established by James Britten (a convert), in order to pursue Cardinal Newman's hope of developing an educated Catholic laity. Both organisations flourished and were replicated around the English-speaking world, helping to contribute to the sense of Catholicism as a system of ideas worthy of serious consideration.

In a booklet published in 1925 and intended for the training of speakers, Frank Sheed wrote that

> It is only when the Guildsman, knowing the Catholic teaching on any doctrine, knows also what the crowd thinks the Church teaches, and what they have in its place, and why they prefer their own substitute, and how best they may be shown the superiority of the Church's teaching to their own substitute, that he may be said to understand the doctrine for Guild purposes.

How high Sheed's expectation now seems; yet how necessary the task remains.

Understanding Catholicism and imparting it to others takes different forms and can be conducted at different levels; but in an age in which ideas have been vulgarised, or, where they are still taken seriously, seem largely to have become the preserve of the non-religious and the irreligious, it is especially important to encourage intellectual Catholicism. As in other departments of life, however, if there is to be improvement there needs to be example and leadership, and these are now in diminishing supply.

Of course, we have the Catholic press and Catholic publishers; but often, and understandably, they focus on internal church issues, or when they look outwards it tends to be to fellow believers, or to elements within the wider society and culture that they hope will be sympathetic and approving. In his poem 'The Arrest of Oscar Wilde at the Cadogan Hotel', John Betjeman has Wilde complain: 'So you've brought me the latest Yellow Book; And Buchan has got in it now: Approval of what is approved of, Is as false as a well-kept vow.'

A similar complaint might be brought against the forays of Catholics into the field of secular thought. They seek not to challenge the assumptions and values of worldly intellectuals but to assure the secular thinkers that Catholic thought isn't really as extraordinary as they might have been led to believe. This strategy rarely brings good, and deserves the response 'Why, then, be a Catholic?'. John Paul II wrote of how 'sign of contradiction' might be 'a distinctive definition of Christ and of his Church'; and now Pope Benedict is set upon the task of cultural re-evangelisation. That will not be an easy endeavour but even to have a serious chance it will need a new intellectualism among Catholics, and a body of Catholic thinkers prepared to challenge the prevailing secular intellectual culture. To do that they will need better formation than is currently easily available in the fundamentals of Catholic doctrine and in the philosophical methods by which it has been and can again be supported. It is time again for Catholics to engage seriously with real and substantial ideas, and to do so in the tradition and in the spirit of earlier generations who won through to a distinctively Catholic synthesis of faith and reason.

The issue is not simply one of articulating a coherent account of one's own beliefs; it is a matter of defending faith itself, for no one interested in the position of religion within Western culture and society can fail to be aware that it is now under fairly sustained attack. On the one hand there are those who argue that the values of political liberalism: freedom of thought and expression, toleration and respect for persons, are all threatened by authoritarian, dogmatic, religiously identified communities. On the other, there are atheist critics such as Daniel Dennett and Sam Harris in America and Richard Dawkins and Anthony Grayling in Britain who maintain that quite apart from any social and political implication, religion as such is a malign force, shaping minds through superstition and fantasy and inhibiting the power of reason.

Proponents of the second view also press the first, while those who claim only to be concerned with the introduction of religion into the social field would require believers to adopt an attitude to their faiths that would equate it to a private enthusiasm or hobby. While the recent occasion for such demands that religion be confined to private practice has been the spread of Islam to Western Europe, advocates of social secularism have long criticised denominational schooling as divisive and charged Christians with dragging faith into politics.

These 'secularist' and 'scepticist' assertions are familiar and are neither profound not unchallengeable. Yet in Britain they have induced considerable insecurity among believers who regard themselves as otherwise at ease with contemporary society. It is quite common in Britain to hear people say in defence against such criticisms that their religion is a personal thing, a matter of how they choose to live, not a set of controversial claims about the nature of reality or the necessary conditions of salvation, let alone a set of demands about how human beings in general should live.

Without wishing to probe the decency or sincerity of such people I do want to challenge the intellectual feeble-

ness of this response to the critics of religion. Of course
there is nothing new about lukewarm faith, lazy thinking
or comfortable conformism. What is new, however, is that
these vices are now exhibited among those who regard
themselves as educated, thinking believers. It is an interesting question how this has come about. Part of the explanation so far as Roman Catholicism is concerned is the
ambition to be fully part of society, which has made
Catholics cautious of being counter-cultural. Another is
the expansion of higher education, which saw humanities
and social science degrees being awarded to ever-larger
numbers of people on the basis of intellectually dilute
courses in social, cultural, religious, educational and
media studies. Catholics were among the main beneficiaries of these expansions through the elevation of teacher-
training institutions to university college status.

In earlier times training towards teaching had no
particular tendency to weaken students' faith, and they
viewed it, quite properly, as a form of preparation for
entry to an important profession through which they could
also serve their communities. With the ambition of former
training colleges to attain university status, however,
came a corresponding ambition to provide additional
degree programmes, and these tended to be in line with
current secular fashions in social and cultural studies.

Of course, the history of Catholic entry into higher
education and into middle-class society is more complex,
bringing benefits and gains as well as losses. But it is
necessary to observe something about British Catholicism
and urgent to rectify it, namely, that it is decidedly unin-
tellectual, rarely rising above the level of demandingness
of newspaper or magazine journalism.

Such has been the generous spirit of recent ecumenism,
and such the sense of religion in general being under
attack, that Anglicans and Presbyterians who have traditionally been better educated do not give public voice to
their estimate of the contemporary Catholic intellectual
contribution. They would not be honest to their own

critical standards, however, if they did not think that what they have encountered is pretty poor. Certainly when released from the restraints of politeness a number have expressed themselves privately on the matter.

The result of this situation is that Catholics know little about the history of their faith, its distinctive content, its theological, philosophical, literary and artistic products, its traditions of spirituality, the nature and modes of grace, the gravity of sin, and so on. Some of these matters should be known about as part of Catholic cultural literacy, some for the intellectual, aesthetic and spiritual treasures they offer, and others as matters of practical religion: truths necessary for salvation.

Ill-formed in faith, unrigorous in thought, and socially-conformist in disposition, the new Catholic middle classes have little interest in intellectual enquiry or in confronting serious challenges, especially one's directed at their own faith. The fading fashion for talk of social justice, and the new found favour of environmental concern, are not exceptions to this. Quite the contrary, they are welcomed as topics of concern which have the merit of being endorsed by current secular orthodoxy.

These matters are before my mind in part because of looking again at some of the outstanding creative work and critical thinking of Catholics of the first half of the twentieth century; but also and more relevantly because I recently spent a week divided between Moscow and Rome. It began at the Russian Academy of Sciences with discussions between mainly Continental Catholics and Russian Orthodox; and continued with me speaking to a meeting of European university professors in which several hundred Catholics from across the whole of Europe participated.

As with most gatherings, the two sets of proceedings varied in interest and quality, but unmistakeable was the depth of knowledge about and personal commitment to Catholic faith, culture and thought in its Western and Eastern variants. Also striking was the evidence of extensive contributions to faith-inspired and faith-informed academic writing, journalism, broadcasting and publishing. A similar story can be told about the United States. In Britain, by contrast, the situation is inexcusably poor and it does not pass without notice abroad.

There are some good things going on but they do not constitute an integrated and flourishing intellectual culture. Bishops are rightly concerned about providing priests for the Catholic population, but without intellectual leadership and sound formation that population will continue to diminish, rendered weak by indifference, comfortable in conformism, and intellectually and spiritually unfit to withstand the attacks of secularists and sceptics. The seed has grown weak, the salt has lost its flavour, and the leaders are growing old. Unless efforts are made to rectify the situation, in ten years time there may be no such thing as British Catholic intellectual culture.

15.

Europe and the future of Christian humanism

On 16 July 1997, in what was hailed as an 'historic announcement', Jacques Santer, then President of the European Commission, presented *Agenda 2000* to the European Parliament in Strasbourg. The most widely reported element of this at the time was the news that five former Communist countries, together with Cyprus, had achieved the necessary economic and political reforms to allow accession talks to begin in January of the following year.

In his statement to the parliament Santer observed that 'Enlargement represents an historic turning point for Europe, an opportunity that it must seize for the sake of its security, its economy, its culture and its status in the world.' Political discussion of European matters tends to focus on economic, defence and narrowly political considerations, but the cultural ones may be no less significant. Indeed, in the longer term they may prove to be of primary importance. In any case, it is a mistake to treat economics, politics and culture as if they were distinct elements.

The prospect introduced by *Agenda 2000* was of the enlargement of the EU from fifteen to twenty-one states, extending from Ireland in the west to Poland in the east. These two have long been deeply Catholic countries, and in four of the six then proto-members – the Czech Republic, Hungary, Poland, and Slovenia – Catholicism is the main religion. This is also true of nine of the states in the

Union as it was then comprised. In the remaining EU countries, as in the two other applicants (Estonia and Cyprus), the main religious affiliation is either Protestant or Orthodox. Subsequent enlargement has brought the EU to the point where a decade after Santer's statement there are now twenty-seven members of which, historically, fifteen are predominantly Catholic, eight Protestant, and four Orthodox.

It has often been said that European culture is essentially Christian. Usually this is noted in opposition to challenges of secularism and multiculturalism. The claim is that our ethical and social values: respect for persons, justice, democracy, welfare provision and so on, derive historically, and continue to take their meaning from a broadly Judaeo-Christian understanding of human beings and of their place in the world. In Britain this is given as the rationale for according a role to Christianity in the institutions of the state and for favouring it in religious education.

Some go further, however, and claim that Europe is a cultural artefact of Roman Catholicism. They do not mean by this that Europe is a living example of Catholic values, but rather have in mind the following two claims. First, that the morality, politics and culture of Europe have been shaped by the influence of Catholic Christianity operating through the Holy Roman Empire, the medieval Latin Church, and the subsequent Catholic empires and nation-states lying west of the Urals and north of the Caucusus. Second, that while this influence has waned it still makes best sense of common European values.

Certainly, Europe is less a geographical fact than a moral idea. But its ethical foundations and ideals are not so easily characterised. Its oldest mythological origins lie in the classical tale in which Europa, daughter of the King of Tyre is taken off by Jupiter to Crete, and their divinely sired offspring become the 'Europeans'. In contrast to this is the medieval legend according to which following the Great Flood, the world was divided between the sons of

Noah with Japeth and his descendants populating Europe. God's chosen people going forth to fill the earth.

These contrasting myths represent two humanistic ideals of Europe: one rationalistic and secular, taking its inspiration from the worlds of antiquity and the Renaissance; the other revelatory and religious, being a product of medieval Christianity. They also remind us that there is nothing eternally given about any particular notion of Europe. Rather, human beings have fashioned different understandings in different periods and may choose to revive or change these. Christians cannot presume upon historical loyalties but have to win the case for their beliefs, including their social theology. The Churches may propose, but material interests dispose!

The decline of secular humanism as a utopian ideology and rethinking of the traditional assumptions of left and right in European politics have certainly produced a situation in which there is want of moral, spiritual and social guidance. The teachings of Catholicism, and of Christianity more generally, have the potential to satisfy this longing. Yet there is need for greater attention to the intellectual and spiritual work of re-evangelisation, and for imagination and cultural sensitivity in carrying it out. The enlargement of the European Union may assist that process as attention begins to shift from short-term economic questions to ones of cultural and moral identity.

In asking what Europe is, or what it ought to be, it is important to recall that it is the historic site of the birth and renaissance of Western humanism. The first occurrence of a version of the term variously rendered 'humanism', *'umanesimo'*, *'humanismo'*, *'humanisme'*, etc, is in the writings of the German philosopher and educationalist Friedrich Niethammer who speaks of *'humanismus'* in the course of debating the proper form, content and purpose of education. That was in the first decade of the nineteenth century; but of course the source of the word and of the idea it represents lie in the world of classical antiquity. *Humanitas* is the term used by Cicero to render the Greek

notion of *enkyklia paedeia*, which refers to a broad education in what would later come to be termed the liberal arts.

It was the aim of such an education to equip someone
with the knowledge and mental training that would enable
him (then, and for centuries after, it would only have been
a 'him') to interpret and understand human events and to
play a role in human affairs by taking part in civic debate.
If Niethammer was less concerned with the goals of public
life and politics, he was of one mind with the ancients in
thinking that education should be about exploring what is
distinctive to human nature and about realising its highest
powers, rather than for training human beings in purely
instrumental skills. Liberal learning and cultivated sensibility was also the ideal of the Renaissance thinkers to
whom the term 'Humanists' was first applied in the mid-
nineteenth century by the cultural historians George Voigt
and Jacob Burckhardt.

Speaking more broadly, and less historically, humanism
is a general style of thought that interprets significance
and value from the point of view of human needs, interests, sensibilities and practices. That is not to say that
humanism must confine itself to the human, or that it
must think of human beings in individualistic terms. It is
true that the present age is increasingly given to these
approaches, but both historically and from the broad char-
acterisation I have just given of humanism it remains open
whether it may also be religious and whether its account of
the person, its philosophical anthropology, is ineliminably
social.

For Christians any adequate 'humanist philosophy'
must incorporate, or be conjoined with a religious understanding of human nature as something possessed intrinsically of powers of reason, deliberation and free action;
created for the purpose of coming to know, to love and to
serve its creator; and capable of being united to God in a
special way in consequence of the incarnation and atone-
ment, and by means of grace. Evidently these remarks
allude to a distinctive theology, and many who today seek

a new humanism to replace the reductive materialisms, deterministic naturalisms, and instrumentalised views of reason and value that have dominated in recent decades, are not religious believers. One may wonder, therefore, how there can be any serious intellectual co-operation between Christian humanists and others seeking to get beyond contemporary materialist orthodoxies. Here there need not only be one answer; but allow me to make a brief recommendation.

Christian humanists of a philosophical sort have been inclined to emphasise as prior and most urgent the importance of developing a metaphysical theory of the person and an account of the foundation and structure of natural law. I am not at all against such projects per se; indeed they interest me greatly, but there is a danger that in trying to excavate to the deepest ground one never gets to the point of erecting a building, let alone of inhabiting it. And the seeming endlessness and difficulties of the excavation may encourage onlookers to conclude that the task cannot be done. Better then to create what may be less deeply founded structures, yet ones that are according to the same design as the unshakable edifice one would hope eventually to construct.

The point here is that while deep theory is being explored one may yet consider what its evaluative and practical implications would be and begin to implement them. Additionally, if we really believe that there is such a thing as human nature, that it includes intellectual and moral powers, and that it is in some way *imago dei*, an image of God (*immagine di Dio, image de dieu*), then we should have confidence that anyone of good faith who is open to the deliverances of lived experience, and it is not perversely resistant to the inbuilt teleology of creatures seeking their fulfilment, will incline to the same conclusions about the objectivity of truth and the reality of value.

What this introduces is the importance of finding a place for phenomenology in our methods of analysis and reasoning; 'phenomenology' not in any esoteric theory-dependent conception, but in the simple sense of description and interpretation of what presents itself to attentive experience. Here is the place to start in discussion with those seeking a new humanism yet who are hesitant or even resistant to Christian belief. There should be no failure of match between on the one hand a true metaphysics of the person and true theory of the form and content of the natural law; and on the other a true phenomenological description of experienced values and meanings.

With that thought in mind let me return briefly to the issue of European culture. Here again I should caution against simplification and the premature desire for a unifying theory constructed at some great depth. The term 'Europe' bears different kinds of significance: geographical, historical, political and cultural. As we mark fifty years since the original Treaties of Rome, and reflect on the ongoing debates between members of the European Union about its nature and proper role, it is hard to resist the tendency to think of Europe solely in political and economic terms. I have already said that this risks neglecting the cultural meaning of European identity. What must also be said, however, is that it would also be a mistake to suppose that there is a single unifying cultural identity to Europe, or indeed that there ever was such. Greek philosophy, Jewish monotheism, Roman Law and Christian incarnationalism, are of enormous importance but apart from the fact that other elements have featured in the Continent's development, how these four expressed themselves has varied across regions, nations and times. Again I would appeal to the value of reflecting on the diversity of real experience, instead of racing ahead to provide a unitary theoretical account of a distinctively European cultural identity.

Such reflection on real experiences is of value to individuals but it needs to be communicated and shared; and before individuals can be capable of it they need to be educated into various forms and modes of cultural description, interpretation and analysis. That is a central function of universities once routinely heralded as such and honoured in practice. But for reasons with which we are all familiar universities have acquired, and become increasingly to be dominated by, other functions. It is not wrong to ask how does higher education contribute to the economy? Or how can more of the population be equipped for the world in which they will live? It is wrong, however, to think that the answers must dictate educational philosophy. The writer Oliver Goldsmith suggested that the issue of whether a certain policy is correct was resolved by the fact that given certain practicalities people would choose it. To this Dr Samuel Johnson responded 'No, Sir, it does not solve the question. It does not follow that what a man would do is therefore right.' We are in a somewhat similar position. All over Europe higher education is responding to government and commercial pressures by choosing to orient its education towards employment, the economy and leisure, at the cost of sustained disciplined study in arts, humanities and sciences. But this does not solve the question.

Being beneficiaries of an educational tradition forged out of classical culture and Judaeo-Christian thought, Catholic academics should be aware of what it is right to aim for in education, and should have confidence in the power of a coherent and ennobling humanism to commend itself to others who are also seeking to escape cultural and economic materialism. Their task, therefore, should be to engage in discussion, with colleagues, with students and with the wider society, about the nature of intellectual and moral values, and in doing that, and in living and working in accord with those values, to draw others into the sphere of a new humanism that can serve both to secure the place of liberal education or *paideia* in the universities, and of humanistic dispositions in European society more widely. If that seems a large and daunting task then the sooner it is begun, or returned to, the better. As Pope Benedict said in an address in 2007 on the theme of the role of the universities in shaping a new humanism for Europe, the work of 'bringing the light of the Gospel to contemporary culture' is a responsibility for Christian university educators.

Section IV

Ethics, the Church and society

16.

More ethics, less emotion

We are ever more conscious of the importance of the ethical aspects of policy and practice, ever more aware of the complexity of ethical decision making, ever more challenged by seemingly new issues, and yet ever less confident about the moral basis on which to found our actual deliberations and decisions. Some characterise the last aspect by saying that we now live in a moral vacuum, but it would be more accurate to say that our world has become morally overcrowded. It is precisely because so much is now claimed about principles and values, rights and duties, requirements and prohibitions, and is advanced from an ever-wider variety of ethical, philosophical and religious perspectives, that we feel it hard to keep hold of consistent lines of thought.

If we were dealing with trends in fashion it would be possible to live with the situation saying 'each to his and her own', for there would be no need to have agreed common policies. And if the issues were ones that could be solved by consistency alone, like adopting a policy of driving on one side of the road, then we might soon arrive at some effective conventions.

But what social ethics has to deal with is not a matter of taste or convenience: it addresses how we ought to live, what values and principles should inform our policies and practices, what goals we ought to pursue, and what courses, if any, we must always avoid. And since many of the issues we now have to deal with have implications for all of us and are the subject of law, the 'we' is not some sub-group of especially interested professionals, it is the members of society as a whole.

On Maundy Thursday 2005, the Science and Technology Committee of the UK House of Commons published a report on reproductive technologies, reviewing the operation of the *Human Fertilisation and Embryology Act* (1990) and the *HFE Authority* (established to regulate practice and to advise on policy in those areas). The report adopted a 'users' perspective on the issues, and a libertarian approach to reproductive rights: researchers should be free to pursue reproductive cloning and the blending of human and animal cells, and would-be-parents should be free to avail themselves of sex-selection and other genetic services.

Presupposed to this is the idea that in its earliest stages human life is of limited value and may be used in experimentation and for purposes of reproductive enhancement. As the committee chairman, Ian Gibson, remarked 'As long as people are doing it for the right reasons, what is wrong?' Critics were not slow in providing answers. Indeed, more than half of the active committee members took exception to the report, refused to be associated with it, and issued a statement of opposition expressing the view that the it is 'unbalanced, light on ethics, goes too far in the direction of deregulation and is too dismissive of public opinion'.

The general reaction has been similarly hostile, with revulsion expressed at the willingness to treat embryos as instruments for the acquisition of knowledge or for the satisfaction of reproductive preferences. Significant though this opposition is, it leaves open the question of how to deal with the increasing torrent of ethical challenges posed by the development of medical technology and the diversity of attitudes to the manufacture, manipulation and ending of life.

It is with these broader issues in mind, as well as in response to the approach represented by the Committee's

report, that there have been several calls for the establishment of a national UK bioethics committee. That appeal
was given prominence in 2005 by statements issued by
Cardinal Murphy-O'Connor of Westminster and by the
Chief Rabbi Sir Jonathan Sacks. As might be expected,
both proposed that such a committee should include
representation from Britain's faith groups, but the shared
vision is broader, and it was clear from the Cardinal's
statement, and from an associated press release, that a
good deal of thought had been given to the rationale and
remit for such a committee.

The current state of affairs in Britain is bad and is probably getting worse. Politicians have little time and no
special aptitude for deep ethical reflection; and many of
the interest groups that do discuss bioethical issues are
only engaging the like-minded. Agencies such as the
HFEA and the Human Genetics Commission have limited
remits and tend to treat issues in an ad hoc way, in isolation from broader questions of human value, and with
only notional regard for common opinion. If we are to
have any chance of dealing with the problems already
upon us, let alone those lying ahead, we need to develop an
approach to bioethics that is capable of integrating different levels of discussion, across a range of issues, and in
ways that better reflect the consensus, as well as the diversity of opinion to be found in society.

One model for this might be the sort of entity established in the US by Presidential directive. Under President
Clinton, the National Bioethics Advisory Commission got
off to an excellent start when it observed that

> The formation of appropriate public policy with respect to
> [human cloning] depends on more than the potential bene-
> fits and harms ... It also depends on the traditions,
> customs and principles of constitutional law that guide
> public policy making.

Similar sensitivity to the wider normative context has
been shown by Bush's Presidential Bioethics Committee,

but these bodies have features inappropriate to the UK context. First, their membership is directly appointed by the President; second, they operate within the framework of a written constitution; and third, their role has been restricted to consultation and advice, and does not extend to reviewing existing regulations and agencies.

Most European states now have bioethics committees and it is appropriate culturally and politically to look to the Continent, as well as to the US, for elements that might be incorporated in a UK institution. The German example is particularly apt, for it involves both a parliamentary committee and a national forum. The former is titled the Study Commission on Ethics in Modern Medicine and is mostly concerned to assist law-makers by providing reports and information on subjects for which legislation may be proposed. Half the twenty-six commissioners are members of the Bundestag and the others are appointed by the political groupings according to proportional representation.

The German National Ethics Council was established in 2001 to serve as a forum for discussion between scientists, medical practitioners, philosophers, theologians, and representatives of law, social theory and economics. Its area of concern is broadly defined as ethical issues pertaining to the life sciences, reflecting in part the strong German interest in environmentalism. More immediately relevant than its scope is its inclusive character and public orientation. It is required to engage with the public and it is significant that its reports reflect a more protective attitude to human life.

It is ironic, therefore, that while members of the HFEA and similar groupings have been unsure what to make of the call for a national bioethics committee, the Society for Protection of Unborn Children issued a statement condemning the Cardinal's proposal:

> SPUC strongly opposes [the Cardinal's] call to the government and parliament to set up a national bioethics

commission ... [such a] commission will prove to be the
graveyard of pro-life ethical concerns ... We need to
ensure that the House of Commons ... reflects the public's
concern that the sanctity of life be respected ... If lethal
experiments were being carried out on Anglicans,
Catholics and Jews, would it be appropriate for religious
leaders to call for a commission to discuss the matter?

This response is multiply flawed. First, it overlooks the
fact that pro-life voices have been effective in getting their
concerns into public consciousness. Most successful in
this regard is CORE (Comment on Reproductive Ethics)
whose director, Josephine Quintavalle, was among the
first to call for a national bioethics committee. Second,
while parliamentarians have much to distract their attention and to pull at their affiliations, a bioethics committee
might be better able to see things in an impartial light and
its membership might be more easily subject to parliamentary scrutiny reflective of the public's general
concerns. Third, the concluding analogy is misconceived
as well as unhelpfully provocative. Efforts to see policy put
on a better ethical foundation are not sectarian but univer-
salist, and are motivated by the belief that a better quality
of shared discussion is more likely to produce a change in
policy than is the repeated denunciation of politicians and
scientists.

Precisely because US and European national bioethics
committees reflect broad lines of division within society
they struggle to arrive at agreed conclusions; but that is
not discreditable or fruitless, for it is better to register the
difficulties than to ignore or deny them. As things stand
much thinking about moral questions in the public sphere
is confused, confusing and increasingly devoid of deep
content. We need to establish a shared means of thinking
seriously, openly, and respectfully of common opinion,
about such matters. The HFEA and parliamentary
committees have proved inadequate to the task, showing
themselves to be at odds with public thinking and arrogant
in choosing to ignore it.

Writing in the *Tablet* ('Talking Ethics', 4 June, 2005)
Richard Harries the Anglican Bishop of Oxford responded
to the call for a UK national bioethics committee, referring
to my own previous proposal of this in the *Tablet* and *The
Times*. He wrote as if the problem with the existing situation was that pro-lifers lacked representation on existing
bodies, such as the two of which he was then a member:
the HFEA and the Nuffield Council on Bioethics. He
suggested that some expanded version of the former might
be able to accommodate them while they could seek
membership of the latter for themselves. He also conceded
the need to review the operations of the HFEA and the
HFE Act.

Interesting as these concessions may be they failed to
address the broader points. The conduct of regulatory
agencies and the issues surrounding human reproduction
are but examples of a much wider range of concerns. Likewise the matter of membership of private committees or
study groups is, though significant, of secondary importance. I served on the Nuffield Council Working Party on
Genetics and Mental Disorder and was impressed by the
seriousness with which the Council conducts its business.
I was also a member of the editorial board of the *Journal
of Medical Ethics* for a decade and noted the sincerity of
academics and clinicians. None of this, however, weakens
the case for a national bioethics committee.

Bishop Harries' repeated reference to the position of
'pro-life advocates' echoes an observation often voiced in
private and occasionally let slip in public, namely that the
inclusion of pro-lifers – interestingly the term often used
is '[Roman] Catholics' – would make the workings of a
committee near to impossible. This is some kind of objection to the establishment of a national bioethics committee but hardly a creditable or publicly defensible one.
Moreover, precisely because US and European national
bioethics committees reflect broad lines of division within
society they struggle to arrive at agreed conclusions; but
that is not discreditable or fruitless, for it is better to

register the difficulties than to ignore or deny them. Also, when one course is refused it is more likely that others will be discovered that can secure greater consensus – as, indeed, is proving to be the case in the field of stem-cell research.

Following a public consultation on the operation of the HFEA the HFE Act, and the HTA (Human Tissue Authority), the UK Government published the 2007 Human Tissue and Embryos (Draft) Bill. Parliament then appointed a Joint Committee of the Lords and Commons to review the proposed legislation. In oral and written evidence I and others repeated the calls and arguments for a National Bioethics Committee and in their Recommendations the Joint Committee write as follows:

> 295. Ultimately it must be for Parliament to set the ethical framework, taking the widest range of advice. We consider that an ethical input should be found from within Parliament and we recommend that Parliament should establish a joint bioethics committee of both Houses to provide ethical input to legislation raising significant issues in bioethics, such as the current draft bill.

Perhaps this represents some progress though it fails to address the point that politicians have little time, and no particular aptitude for deep ethical analysis and deliberation. The argument for a UK National Bioethics Committee remains and the case is practical as well as principled: that should be a persuasive combination, and in time I hope it will prove so.

17.

Sexuality, ethics and politics

Writing at the time of the debate surrounding the repeal of the famous Section 28 clause in local government legislation prohibiting the promotion of homosexuality, the Scottish political journalist Iain McWhirter wrote that the country 'must never return to the dark ages of homophobia'. He continued 'The Section 28-ers insist they have nothing against homosexuals as such ... it's just that they don't want their practices presented as acceptable and morally equivalent to heterosexual ones.' Though this was offered in a spirit of sarcasm it is, I think, accurate to the majority view and represents a position that is far from evidently extreme. MacWhirter went on to say, probably fairly, that the purpose of Clause 28 was 'to prevent homosexuality being regarded as normal' and that it '[banned] the teaching of homosexuality as an acceptable and natural form of relationship'.

The general suggestion is that anyone who takes this view is guilty of unjust discrimination and, more accusingly, that anyone who thinks homosexual practice is not acceptable thereby shows themselves to be homophobic. A more honest and better informed commentary would recognise that there are seriously disputed questions of justice and morality at issue which cannot be resolved by stipulative definition and name-calling. In truth, the motives and reasons of those opposing repeal were many and various and included, in some cases, an irrational fear or loathing of homosexuals. But no serious, educated person could suppose that this is the sole or even main ground of opposition. The obvious fact is that many people believe that homosexual practice is wrong, and while they would not wish to see anyone persecuted or prosecuted for what is done by consenting adults in private, nor do they wish this to be represented publicly as morally acceptable, particularly not in schools.

These attitudes are open to challenge and they are not beyond all reasonable doubt, but it is alarming to think that the very expression of them may be becoming an occasion for abusive denunciation. Following the vote of Anglican bishops in the 1998 Lambeth Conference on the issue of homosexuality and Christian teaching, I was contacted by a Sunday newspaper to give my view of the matter as a Roman Catholic and as a philosopher. My initial reaction was to decline the invitation since it seemed presumptuous to speak as a non-Anglican about matters internal to that communion. However, it emerged that what was wanted was a Catholic view of the issue of homosexual practice. I commented and my observations were duly reported though, for reasons of space, as a series of assertions rather than arguments.

On the very same day, another philosopher — Professor Anthony O'Hear — found himself called upon as a member of the BBC Radio 4 *Any Questions* panel to comment on the Lambeth decision. O'Hear is not a Christian and he made it clear that he was not in a position to invoke the biblical and theological beliefs of the orthodox bishops. Nonetheless he judged that from a traditional Christian perspective the rejection of homosexual activity, as of *any* sexual activity outside marriage, is inescapable. This met with jeers from the audience and provoked another panel member into a bout of intense moral indignation to the effect that such views as the orthodox bishops propounded, and to which O'Hear seemed to give some kind of respectability, were deeply morally offensive.

Since my own press comments endorsed the conclusions of the Lambeth majority I found myself liable to the same charge of not merely tolerating the intolerable but of advocating it. What I find interesting about this is that the view of the Lambeth majority and of many others who have thought hard about these issues is based on a philosophical perspective of great antiquity which until quite recently was widely invoked among educated people. It may be of use, therefore, if I set out in brief the basis of the traditional Christian view (similar views are held by Jews, Muslims and many agnostics and atheists).

One strictly religious argument is that the Hebrew Bible explicitly denounces homosexual practice, that this is nowhere contradicted in the teachings of Jesus Christ, and that it is repeated in the letters of St Paul. Someone who now wishes to defend the legitimacy of homosexual activity will have to say that what Jews and Christians regard as the inspired Word of God is false on a matter of unquestionable importance. Non-Christians may greet this opportunity with enthusiasm, but scriptural consensus is not something that believers can treat lightly as they might strict dietary and sabbatarian regulations which evidently do not enjoy cross-testamental support.

In the same paper in which my comments were reported the Right Revd Michael Hare Duke, former Episcopalian Bishop of St Andrews, expressed his opposition to the Lambeth decision saying

> There is nothing that should exclude people from the full life of the Church. The Early Church had difficulty in establishing itself as a boundary free zone. St Paul fought a battle to say that there should be 'neither Jew nor Greek, neither male nor female, nether bond nor free'.

First, it is surely obvious that some things do and should cause a person's exclusion from the full life of the Church, namely unrepented sin and public disregard for the Church's fundamental teachings. Second and relatedly, Paul's remarks concern the universality of Christ's redemptive mission; but the possibility of forgiveness and salvation turn on recognition of fault and acceptance of Christ's injunction to go and sin no more. Third, it is Paul who is the most vocal first Christian critic of homosexual activity.

So much for scripture. Moral theology has traditionally made appeal to a different source in arguing against homosexual activity, namely the natural law. Interestingly, when I mentioned this fact to a journalist there came the reply 'what is that?' The idea of the natural law pre-dates Christianity and versions of it are found in different systems of ancient thought, such as those employed in Greece by Aristotle, in Rome by Cicero, and in China by the author of the *Tao Te Ching*. In essence, it is the idea that human actions may be judged good (or bad) according to whether they promote or contribute to (inhibit or damage) natural human flourishing. This last notion is explicated in terms of the realisation of potentialities that are definitive of human beings as such. So, for example, we have certain biological, psychological and social needs, the fulfilment of which is necessary for our well-being. If I am starved, denied relaxation or refused human contact I suffer; if I am fed, rested and kept company then, other things being equal, I am liable to flourish.

Now I turn to sex. According to the natural law, judgements as to the moral acceptability of sexual practices must be keyed to an understanding of the proper role of sex in human life; and what reason teaches is that this role is primarily — though not exclusively — one of reproduction. Suppose a group of alien beings, or members of a hitherto unknown species of earthly animal, were discovered and scientists were interested in understanding their nature. How would they determine whether the animals had eyes? They would shine lights and move objects around the beings checking for signs of light sensitive reactions. How would they determine whether these beings had sexual organs? By seeing whether activity involving any particular parts resulted in the production of offspring. In short sexual organs are defined by function and their (primary) function is that of reproduction.

What follows from this is that the primary definitive use of sexual organs is inter-sexual, between male and female, and for the sake of reproduction. Does it also follow that this is the only legitimate use? I do not think so. Consider the analogy with eating. The organs of this are the mouth and digestive tract. Accordingly their primary definitive use is to consume food for the benefit of the body in general. Is this the only reason to eat? Evidently not. There is also the pleasure of savouring the taste and texture of one's meal as there is the pleasure of sharing the table with others. Nonetheless, someone who divorced the practice of putting food in their mouth from the process of digesting it would be – and ought to be – judged perverse. Eating and spitting out, or vomiting up, adopted as general practices are pathological conditions.

The same holds good in the sexual case. I am not arguing that the only function of sex or of the sexual organs is to reproduce. Sex obviously gives pleasure and serves to express and deepen emotional bonds; but these features are conjoined to its primary function which is reproductive. The claim that sex is essentially keyed to reproduction is neither more nor less puzzling than the analogous claim that eating is essentially keyed to taking nourishment. Yet denial of the former is precisely what is implied by the suggestion that sexual orientation is an option. Of course one may opt never to digest food taken orally, but that decision expresses a form of natural disorder and will lead to trouble. Likewise, the option of anal intercourse is there for those who choose it, but in doing so they are choosing perversely — and that is equally true whether the partners are male/male or male/female.

Am I arguing, therefore, for the Roman Catholic view that contraceptive or otherwise non-generative activity among heterosexuals is also contrary to the natural law. Not as such, and I think this teaching goes beyond what can be established on the basis of non-theological premises. Consider again the case of eating. While it would be perverse never to eat for nutrition's sake and always to regurgitate digested food, it does not follow that each and every occasion of eating must be directed towards nutrition. One might, indeed, have occasions on which food was sampled for its flavour but not consumed. Even so, the primary function of eating remains that of consuming food. And the primary function of sexual activity remains that of reproduction. Homosexual activity like the intentional consumption of indigestible material or the continuing and deliberate regurgitation of food is a misuse of natural human capacities. How serious a misuse is not a matter I feel competent to judge.

I hope that those who disagree with what I have written may nonetheless accept that it presents a serious and sincerely held position, one far removed from homophobia. We all struggle with inclinations we did not choose and often wish we did not have, that is one of the mysteries of the human condition. It is Christian wisdom to recognise this fact and Christian charity to help one another deal with it. Of course Christian thought and practice are in decline in Western liberal societies and it may be on this account that natural law reasoning is increasingly unfamiliar, and also that debate is conducted – even among Christians – with ever less charity or clarity.

Returning to the matter of Section 28 it is worth recording that the letter of guidance advising of the meaning and implications of the 1988 Local Government act (S.O. Circular 9/9/88) writes as follows:

> Local authorities will not be prohibited by this section from offering the full range of their services to homosexuals, on the same basis as to all inhabitants of their areas. So long as they are not setting out to promote homosexuality they may, for example, include in their public libraries books and periodicals about homosexuality or written by homosexuals, and fund theatre and other arts events with homosexual themes ... Sex education will continue to be an element of social and health education in schools.

> Section 28 does not affect the activities of teachers. It will
> not prevent the objective discussion of homosexuality in
> the classroom or the counselling of pupils concerned about
> their sexuality.

Reading this it is hard to see how senior politicians,
including the then Prime Minister, Tony Blair, could say
that Section 28 prevented teachers from doing their job in
educating children about sex and in protecting the vulnerable from bullying; or how commentators and prominent
literary figures could write that the law means that access
is denied to important modern classics which deal with
homosexual themes. Of course, they might have been
ignorant of the law and the guidelines concerning its scope
but if so, then their comments were irresponsible if not
disingenuous.

That said, there is ground for complaint that the clause
was discriminatory in singling out one particular sexual
group. So far as public opinion is concerned it is hard to
suppose that those who maintain the moral superiority of
heterosexual over homosexual activity would be happy to
have local authorities promote sadomasochism or
fetishism. And if that is not the case then the charge of
homophobia does indeed begin to look justified.

What is in fact the case is that most people do not want
local authorities or schools to promote, recommend or
celebrate any particular form of sexual activity though
they would, I suspect, be happy and indeed wish to see
heterosexual marriage, or at least stable, domestic heterosexual family life presented as a desirable norm. Clearly,
though, this would be unacceptable to sexual radicals.
Moreover, they will regard mere social toleration of homosexuality (or of other alternatives) as insufficient, noting
(correctly) that toleration is compatible with moral disap-
proval. But approval cannot be coerced, and it is evident
that the majority do not regard all forms of sexual activity
as 'equally valid'. If pressed as to why they think this they
will usually speak in terms of what is normal or natural.

Such replies are now regularly countered by the suggestion that while homosexuality or fetishism may be statistically abnormal they occur in nature and hence cannot be objected to as unnatural. Whether by accident or design, however, such rejoinders confuse two senses of the terms involved. 'Normal' may mean usual (i.e. according to a pattern), or it may mean conforming to an appropriate standard. Likewise 'natural' may mean not artificial, or according to design or proper function. In each case it is the latter meaning that is intended by the critic of alternative sexualities and his or her position is untouched by pointing out that these occur 'in nature'. So too do inclinations to obsession and addiction but that is hardly a basis for maintaining equivalence between these and the human norm.

Of course such reasoning is unlikely to persuade those who maintain the moral equivalence of all forms of sexual lifestyle. And against this background of fundamental moral disagreement the liberal idea of state neutrality may have some appeal. But it is neither practical, nor consistent with our general view of the state. Morality does and should constrain the public sphere in so far as policies bear upon basic rights and interests. The state exists in part to promote the common good, and more fundamentally to protect its members from harm or injury to their interests arising from the actions of others. On this at least many moral conservatives and radicals are likely to agree.

Discrimination in law on the basis of private sexual practice cannot be justified. On the other hand society has a right to expect its commonly shared interests to be protected, and these include the norm of heterosexual marriage, particularly as that bears upon the needs and formation of children. At the time of the parliamentary debate in the House of Lords, Lord Brightman, and others advanced the following as a proposed replacement for the offending clause:

Subject to the general principal that the institution of
marriage is to be supported, a local authority shall not
encourage or publish material intended to encourage the
adoption of any particular sexual lifestyle. This section
does not prohibit the provision for young persons of sex
education or counselling services on sexual behaviour and
associated health risks.

That was a wise measure and had it been adopted future
controversies might have been avoided.

18.

Scandal in the American Church

One of the reasons why in recent times the Roman Catholic Church has found it difficult to receive a respectful hearing for its teachings on sex is that it is seen as being itself an institution in which sexual wrongdoing is rampant. That is a cruel and unjust verdict but it is encouraged by the scandals of priestly abuse and nowhere have those been more publicly exposed than in the United States.

The Catholic Church in America is indeed in serious trouble. No proper interest is served by pretending otherwise, or by suggesting that this is a storm that will soon pass. The causes of the difficulties remain and the effects will extend for years to come and be felt beyond America itself.

The immediate issue is that of sexual vice among clergy and religious, and the failure of bishops and superiors to take adequate measures against wrongdoers, and to protect the innocent from being preyed upon by them. Quite apart from their moral and religious responsibilities these authorities failed to report criminal activities. So we have the sorry state of multiple offenders being exposed and in some cases imprisoned, and of bishops, archbishops and cardinals being roundly condemned from within as well as outwith the Church.

Certainly the media has been in a frenzied state as they tasted hot blood and wanted more, and all sorts of opportunists have leapt forward to take advantage of the situation; but the truth is that men of the cloth have failed the Church in ways and on a scale that has caused and continues to cause great damage. The image of a hierarchy concerned to protect itself and the Church even at great cost to innocents has been overlain by accusations of earlier papal complicity with Nazism and lack of concern for the Jews. Although these events are separated by time and space the general impression is of a failed organisation letting down those of its own members as well as the wider world – an ecclesial Enron.

Like their Irish counterparts many members of the American hierarchy now feel unable to challenge society over its values and policies, and the prophetic voice of Catholicism is growing weaker. Others seek the favour of their very critics and redirect the blame upwards, suggesting that it is time for the Church to review its understanding of certain fundamentals of religious and moral practice. This is a code for questioning priestly celibacy, an exclusively male priesthood, and sexual ethics, including attitudes to extramarital sex, contraception and homosexuality.

It is common to read that the matter of priestly and religious abuse is not a gay issue but one of paedophilia. This is unconvincing. Most of the cases of sexual vice among clergy involve homosexual approaches and acts involving teenage boys. There have been cases of heterosexual paedophilia but the major problem is homosexual ephebophilia (the attraction of adults to adolescents, as opposed to (pre-pubertal) children) and even this seems to be a matter of clergy taking opportunities with adolescent boys because of lesser risk of exposure than might be posed by soliciting adults. This is one reason why activists are keen that sexual vice not be deemed a gay issue: they hope for acceptance of homosexual activity among religious (i.e., those who have taken vows) and don't want that imperilled by widespread repugnance at what is now being revealed.

In a sincere effort to exercise pastoral sensitivity and in

response to charges of homophobia, senior church figures have emphasised that the Church does not condemn homosexual orientation – only homosexual acts. Though theologically sound this is a confused message and encourages the reaction that if the first is acceptable how can acting on that orientation be wrong. Herein there is a confusion, or at least insufficient distinction between orientation and disposition. The determining forces of sexual orientation are still not well understood, but let us suppose that nature and nurture combine to establish a certain sexual orientation. Between this and habitual action lies disposition.

If one has a certain orientation this need not lead to active sexual practice and whether it does or not depends on the development or inhibition of dispositions. To be disposed is to be primed to act or react in certain ways. So if one has a particular orientation but does not wish to find oneself acting or being strongly inclined to act in accord with it then one needs to attend to one's dispositions. This is where the Church's teaching and its training have tended to be negligent. What should be said to those entering the celibate life is that while their orientations may not matter their dispositions certainly do. Whether heterosexually, homosexually or otherwise oriented they must cultivate strong counter-dispositions to act on these. In other and older words they must cultivate sexual asceticism.

Some current American estimates suggest that perhaps fifty per cent of those training for religious life are of homosexual orientation, and high figures have been speculated about for the situation elsewhere. Obviously this figure or even half of it is greatly disproportionate to the percentage of homosexuals in the population at large. Why should this be so? Two answers suggest themselves. First that the religious life is becoming one of the 'gay' professions. Second that apart from its positive attraction for homosexuals it is losing its appeal for heterosexual men. The latter possibility may have some connection with celibacy which is increasingly at odds with highly sexualised secular lifestyles. But it is also likely to relate to the fact that the priesthood once offered rare opportunities, e.g. of higher education and institutional security, that are more generally available to now affluent members of those historically underprivileged communities from which vocations were drawn.

In the discussions about celibacy one issue that has been overlooked is that an argument from the legitimacy of sexual orientation being expressed in sexual activity, conjoined with the acceptance of the legitimacy of homosexual orientation, yields the conclusion that active homosexuality is compatible with the priesthood. The only principled way to resist the conclusion is to argue from the claim that the proper meaning and role of sexuality includes, if it is not exhausted by, its generative function. On this account dispositions to non-generative sexual acts, and orientations towards such activity are intrinsically disordered.

So we find ourselves heading towards the old controversy over contraception. This is not the occasion to pursue that, but the issues are linked and a decent theology of sex needs to show the extent and nature of that linkage. In the meantime the bishops, religious superiors, and directors of seminaries need to attend to the threefold distinction: orientation, disposition and activity, and to establish a barrier so as to inhibit the occurrence of the third. That wall needs to be placed after orientation, for by the time dispositions have developed it is likely to be too late to prevent their expression in activity; or certainly difficult to counter that tendency.

In many cases it is too late and only heroic corrective efforts assisted by grace will enable individuals to curtail their active proclivities. Their superiors, some of whom may themselves be in the same moral danger, need to encourage asceticism, to insist upon it in the seminaries and to require the departure of those who are unable or unwilling to take the necessary measures, either as staff or students. One reason for reluctance, additional to possible compromise and fear of controversy, is the concern over the perilously low number of vocations. It is hard to predict outcomes but I suspect that a determined treatment of the issue of sexual disposition – homosexual and heterosexual – with effective ascetical training would in fact make the priesthood and religious life more attractive to those of well-ordered sexual character. One might also hope that as it became known that having had this problem the Church had dealt with it, the priesthood might again enjoy the prestige that once gave it a kind of nobility.

At any rate no good outcome can be hoped for until this painful nettle has been grasped. And as is so often the case the task will be made easier and the remedy more likely to be effective by the cultivation of spiritual virtues. The French Jesuit Jean Pierre de Caussade lived in the eighteenth century, in a period and in a country that had also seen sexual scandals in the seminaries and among the religious. In a work compiled from his letters of spiritual counsel and given the title *Self-Abandonment to Divine Providence* he writes:

> If the business of becoming holy seems to present insufferable difficulties, it is merely because we have a wrong idea about it. In reality holiness consists of one thing only: complete loyalty to God's will. Now everyone can practice this loyalty, whether actively or passively.
>
> To be actively loyal means obeying the laws of God and the church and fulfilling all the duties imposed upon us by our way of life. Passive loyalty means that we lovingly accept all that God sends us at each moment of the day.

It is hard to resist that thought that had churchmen been more attentive to their spiritual reading and to living out its teachings then the scandals of the present day, as of De Caussade's time, might not have been so many or so terrible.

19.

Attending to the faithful in matters of chastity

Following the furore in the early months of 2007 surrounding the Catholic Church's policies on gay adoption, a statement by the Diocese of Westminster 'concerning its outreach and ministry to homosexual persons' provided further occasion for critical comments on church teaching from within Catholic circles. It would be understandable, therefore, if feeling somewhat beleaguered, the Church sought to play down its teachings or to placate its internal critics. These, though, would be mistakes: the first a failure of intellectual integrity and moral virtue, the second an act of imprudence and injustice.

The Westminster statement speaks of the Diocese having become increasingly conscious of particular pastoral needs present in parts of London's West End, and more precisely of the desire of 'a number of homosexual Catholics, together with their parents, families and friends, for pastoral care'. In response, after setting out church teaching on these matters, and noting that Masses serving these interests have been taking place in Islington, and in Soho (at the Anglican Church of St Anne's), the Diocese proposes as part of 'its Pastoral outreach to homosexual people' a bi-monthly Mass to be held at Our Lady of the Assumption in Warwick Street, Soho.

The Masses at St Anne's have been running since July 2005, arranged by the 'Soho Masses Pastoral Council' (SMPC) for 'lesbian, gay, bisexual, transgendered Catholics, and their parents, families and friends'. It is out of discussions between the Diocese and the SMPC that the recent initiative has emerged (though no mention of this group is made in the announcement). A response by the SMPC is given in its own statement of 4 February 2007 'Our Places at the Table' which while expressing satisfaction at 'an agreement that [these Masses] will particularly welcome LGBT Catholics, their parents and their families' takes issue with its use of the language and substance of traditional Catholic moral teachings.

The diocesan initiative recognises the pastoral needs of some of those upon whom the Church's longstanding teaching on sexuality may rest heavily. Well-intended, therefore, and explicit in maintaining church teachings, it nevertheless gives rise to certain risks. First, of encouraging or even recognising sectionalist interest; second, of confusing and giving scandal to the faithful; third, of undermining the efforts of those who, though of homosexual inclination, strive to live according to the Church's teachings and seek no special privileges; and fourth, of compromising the conduct of the Mass and the gift of the Eucharist.

Many of those involved in the SMPC are opposed to church teaching in these matters and choose to participate in the sacramental life of the Church on their own terms and not in respectful fidelity to its teachings. Bidding prayers used in the Soho Masses celebrate and seek blessing for same-sex unions following their civil partnerships.

It is said by internal critics of church teaching that there is a diversity of theological reflection on the matter of human sexuality in particular in relation to sexually expressed same-sex attraction. It is also said that the authority of church teaching depends upon its reception and upon the *sensus fidelium*. These claims seem often to be advanced either in ignorance or with the intention of undermining traditional understandings.

From the Council of Jerusalem, the Church has promulgated essentially the same teaching on matters of sexual practice, and there simply is no other body of conciliar, catechetical or magisterial teaching at odds with this (see the historical references to the *Declaration on Certain Questions Concerning Sexual Ethics*, 1975). Also the *sensus* and *consensus fidelium* are not like the responses to a political opinion poll or social survey trend. They presuppose faithful participation in the life of the Church and have to be considered not in one time and place but across all times and all places.

The question, therefore, is not 'What do secularised Catholics living in Britain or Western Europe, and deeply immersed in its values, think?' but 'What have the faithful over the centuries and across the continents thought and lived?' Some of the recent critical commentary cites the name of Newman as if in support of change, but this only shows their ignorance of what Newman said and wrote (most relevantly in 'On Consulting the Faithful in Matters of Doctrine').

The risks of confusing and giving scandal to the faithful, and of exploitation of the gift of the Mass are obvious enough, but equally important is the seeming failure to give explicit support for groups that do seek to live in accord with Church teaching, groups such as *Courage* and *Encourage*. The aims of *Courage* are defined by its five goals:

Chastity: Live chaste lives in accordance with the Roman Catholic Church's teaching on homosexuality.

Prayer and Dedication: Dedicate one's life to Christ through service to others, spiritual reading, prayer, meditation, individual spiritual direction, frequent attendance at Mass, and the frequent reception of the Sacraments of Reconciliation and the Holy Eucharist.

Fellowship: Foster a spirit of fellowship in which all may share thoughts and experiences and so ensure that no one will have to face the problems of homosexuality alone.

Support: Be mindful of the truth that chaste relationships are not only possible but necessary in a chaste encouragement to one another in forming and sustaining them.

Good Example: Live lives that may serve as good examples to others.

These noble Christian goals are heroically pursued by members of *Courage* and others, and it was a missed opportunity in a statement on outreach and ministry to homosexual persons not to express explicit appreciation of those who seek to live in accord with the Church's teachings, and not to acknowledge the good work of organisations such as *Courage*. It must be saddening for members of these to see groups hostile and unfaithful to the Church's teachings given attention while they who strive to live in accord with the only teaching that has ever been promulgated by the Church go unacknowledged, let alone praised.

It would be fitting, therefore, if the Westminster Diocese were to take an early opportunity publicly to differentiate between homosexual groups opposed and others faithful to Church teaching, and in particular to quote and commend the five goals of courage: *Chastity, Prayer and Dedication, Fellowship, Support,* and *Good Example*; all pursued in line with the one, ancient, universal and continuing teaching of the Church that sexual activity belongs exclusively within the marital union of one man and one woman.

In times of opposition and contradiction, when other difficulties afflict the Church, it can seem opportune to attend sympathetically to critics, but prudence and justice dictate honouring the faithful and the loyal, for they are the life of the Church in season and out of it, whose faith and practice give meaning to the expression *sensus fidelium.*

Afterword

In the week following the publication in the *Tablet* of the article from which the foregoing is drawn, the Vicar General of the Diocese of Westminster, Mgr Seamus Boyle, wrote to the paper (10 March 2007) 'to emphasise' that

The announcement concerning these Masses made clear the Church's teaching that sexual intercourse finds its proper place and meaning in marriage alone. The Church does not share the assumption that every adult person needs to be sexually active. Every person, whether homosexual or heterosexual, is called to chastity. They are helped to do this through friendship, prayer and sacramental grace. Homosexual people are rightly given pastoral care within their own parishes. It is the expectation of the Cardinal that all who attend these Masses in Soho wish to live in full communion with the Church and also strive to live by the Church's moral teachings. While the Church continues to uphold objective moral norms, it is also wise, compassionate and understanding of the difficult challenge that many experience in living the kind of chaste life to which the Lord calls us.

This is an admirable statement blending moral theology with pastoral concern; and it deserves to be attended to wherever similar issues arise.

20.

Future trends in Christian ethics in Europe

In May 2006 almost fifty of us assembled in the Schloss Wilhelminenberg in Vienna for an historic meeting. Our host was Cardinal Schonborn, Archbishop of Vienna and president of the Trustees of the Pro Oriente Foundation established in 1964 by Cardinal Konig to promote mutual understanding between Eastern and Western Christians. In recognition of its potential value and importance beyond the confines of Europe the event was co-sponsored from the United States by the Lynde and Harry Bradley Foundation.

We were gathered under the joint presidency of their Eminences Metropolitan Kyril of Smolensk and Kaliningrad, Chairman of the Department of External Church Relations of the Moscow Patriarchate, and Cardinal Poupard, President of the Pontifical Council for Culture and the Pontifical Council for Inter-Religious Dialogue, and with the blessings of their Holinesses Patriarch Alexis II and Pope Benedict XVI. Our purpose was to initiate a joint Orthodox/Catholic dialogue on the theme of the *Mission and Responsibility of the Churches* with regard to the moral, cultural and spiritual condition of Europe. Overall, the three-day meeting was a success and issued in a joint statement which included the following:

We are concerned for the destiny of European nations and
their role in the modern world. While the Orthodox and
Catholic traditions belong to the same European civiliza-
tion, their influence led to the formation of distinctive
cultures on the European continent and in other parts of
the world. We are united not only by a religious, historical
and cultural heritage, but also by an identical view of the
way in which contemporary public and private life should
be arranged ...

It is only a solid combination of the principles of
freedom and moral responsibility that can help to ensure
Europe's present and future common good.

Those aware of the historic tensions between Orthodox
and Catholic, compounded by the political oppositions
between East and West, and the revival of Russian self-
confidence, will recognise the achievement represented by
this joint statement.

A year later, in June 2007, a second meeting was
convened under the same joint presidency. Held at the
Russian Academy of Sciences in Moscow its theme was
Christianity, Culture and Moral Values. As well as representing the continuation of this new East/West dialogue,
there was a specific continuity in subject matter, for
although the general title of the second conference made
no explicit reference to Europe it remained the principal,
if not the exclusive focus of our attention. One great
benefit of the Vienna meeting had been to highlight the
complex pattern of historical events and processes, of
philosophical and theological ideas, and of moral and spiritual values that constitute European culture in the broad-
est sense of that expression. In that broad sense 'culture'
refers to the experiences, reflections and creations of
peoples from Ireland in the west to Russia in the east;
from Scandinavia in the north to the Mediterranean
islands in the south.

That is a vast expanse, within which there is much diversity, and it would be a mistake to try to reduce the very considerable differences of social, political, artistic, intellectual and

religious history and practice to anything like a unitary, or even a synthesising form. One might think that no one could ever have attempted this. Yet the ambition of unity through sameness has been a recurrent, and destructive motivation in the history of Europe; particularly in the last three centuries, and most especially in the twentieth century. Until the development of modern communications and military technology the pursuit of unity through conquest and governance was either intensive but localised, or extensive but relatively superficial. In the twentieth century, however, the dream of a unitary socio-political order seemed realisable through revolutionary movements, military campaigns and the creation and domination of pan-European markets in goods and services.

These are, of course, very different forces and methods of establishing unity, and their effects and the ways and time-periods over which they have been pursued are also quite different. Yet in each case the dream of unity has had the result of inducing alienation, disaffection and loss of the sense of a settled identity. Such identity is the principal resource first, for pursuing intellectual and aesthetic projects; second, for developing a sense of moral purpose, self-worth and mutual respect; and third, for coping with the challenges and tragedies that are recurrent in human experience.

This form of human-existential identity presents itself as prior to the life and experience of any individual. It is not, however, an abstract ideal or a general conception, but something concrete and experienceable in particular cultural embodiments. These include patterns of agriculture and fishing, forms of construction, building design, street plans, oral histories, songs, stories, social clubs, organisations, institutions, religious devotions, practices and liturgies, and so on, and so on.

From the point of view of someone seeking to find, or to impose unity these particularities present a challenge. They are deep-rooted and their roots and stems are intertwined. They are objects of local affection and loyalty. They do not conform to any general pattern, and they resist integration within a common scheme or plan. Faced with these facts the searcher after unity who seeks to find or impose this through action must deny the significance of cultural diversity; and since that diversity is to be found at different levels across the range of human interests and practices he must be willing to deny a very great deal. In addition, if unity is to be pursued in practice then what is resistant to it must be contained, perhaps within the private sphere, or destroyed. In fact these may not be alternatives, for cultural realities typically occupy and serve to define the public sphere, and pass continuously into the domestic and personal domains. Thus to deny their public expression and celebration, and to seek to restrict them to private interest is to mutilate and wound them mortally.

So it is that at present traditional forms of education, family relationships, voluntary association and religious practice are threatened by political and economic forces that either seek to marginalise or destroy them, or act in ways that show no respect for them, or which will, foreseeably, lead to their destruction.

This is the case with many economic and commercial practices that view all human interests, activities and creations as tradeable commodities. It is now common to read of companies being purchased with the sole purpose of selling off their property and other assets without regard to the interests of employees. Another example is in the area of commercial advertising where demand is created and cultivated for goods and services which populations do not need, cannot afford and which are damaging to their lives. Levels of personal debt in Europe increase year on year as people struggle to acquire goods the 'need' of which is a result of advertising. These commercial practices erode traditional understandings of what contributes to, and what constitutes human happiness. They also eat into the fabric of personal and family relationships and undermine community life and collective virtue.

This sort of criticism of commodification and market exploitation is a long-familiar complaint of left-wing commentators and activists; but it is interesting to observe how in recent times it has also been voiced by social conservatives who have seen the commercial imperative lead to the destruction of traditional communities and forms of life, in the interest of a unitary culture of consumption, acquisition and display.

Progressives meanwhile have made their own contribution to the destruction of the diverse and complex structures in which generations beyond memory have been introduced to ways of finding meaning and fulfilment. Here I will just mention the example of family life and education. And the point to notice, again, is how the ambition to achieve unity, in this case of values and practices, leads to an attack on areas of resistance.

In 1994, on the occasion of the tenth anniversary of the International Year of the Child, the then Secretary General of the United Nations, Kofi Annan, wrote as follows:

> The family has a continuing and crucial role in social and human development as well as in provision of care and support to individuals. Strong family bonds have always been part of most societies, and families in most places continue to make important contributions to social and economic well-being.

As an affirmation of the value of family life this is welcome, and although Annan does not make the point it is fair to presume that in speaking of 'the family', in full generality, he was mindful of the fact that there is a diversity of forms of family relationship, in some cases with three generations sharing the home, in some with tasks of childrearing being shared among parental siblings with little distinction within the children of the extended family between brothers, sisters and cousins, and so on. This diversity of practices and structures reflects other differences between physical and built environments, patterns of work, material resources and long-standing beliefs and traditions.

Allowing that there may be bad cases, as there are in all things human, the situation of strong families of various sorts contributing to human development, and providing care and support for their members constitutes an example of benign pluralism.

Even at the time when Annan was writing, however, and ever more so since, another rhetoric has developed which also speaks of pluralism, but not in the interest of sustaining traditional forms of family life but with the opposed purpose of undermining them. So it is said by progressives, and defensively echoed by some 'conservatives' who fear being left behind by the ebbing tide of social change, that families come in all shapes and sizes and no form should be privileged. What this means is that those who choose to be single parents; or those who choose to conceive different children with different partners; or those who enter in and out of relationships with children present; or those in same-sex relationships who choose to act as a parent pair, perhaps even resorting to assisted reproduction to have a child: all of these are to be regarded as equally valid to those forms of family life at whose core stand a man and a woman united in lifelong marriage.

I termed the earlier diversity 'benign pluralism' but this is quite different and deserves the description 'pathological pluralism', because not only are the forms I have described departures from a settled social norm, departures that are evidently dysfunctional and damaging to those involved, but the affirmation of them as acceptable is by implication a denial of the special value of marriage as traditionally conceived of in European societies, and in those societies that derive from them. And, having made that move, progressives are often inclined to go further and say that far from being superior to these new arrangements, the traditional European understanding of family is an artefact of oppression, commanding and controlling sexuality in line with heterosexist essentialism, coercing women into reproduction and childrearing, and providing opportunities for the mental and physical abuse of children.

Some of those who say this kind of thing are moral nihilists, or social anarchists, but many see themselves as advocates of a superior, comprehensive moral doctrine, namely that of liberty rights. For these people, the attack on traditional forms and values is part of a constructive revolution designed to implement a unitary moral order in terms of which all institutions, practices, loyalties and relationships may be judged. Earlier I mentioned education as being, along with the family, a target of such attacks. It is unsurprising that these two feature prominently, for they are central to intimate human relationships, and they are primary vehicles for the transmission of values from one generation to the next. Consider then the following from a recent United Kingdom report on children and family policy:

> The absence of a rights approach guiding the relationship between the interests of children and families is significantly in evidence around concessions to that ill-defined attribution parental autonomy which in some circumstances one sees perversely preserved at the expense of children's rights.
>
> . . .
>
> In education, for example, parental choice of school and religious education for their child has been questioned as undermining children's rights ... Overall the Government's role in the parent-child-state axis is to support individuation and opportunity for self-determination and fulfilment. But the relationship is seriously undefined and needs principal clarification.

There are several aspects of this that should be noted. First the idea that family relationships are to be morally assessed through the medium of *rights*. Second, that at present the claims of parents not to be interfered with in the education of their children are *improperly conceded to*. Third, and relatedly, that the exercise of parental choice in the matter of schooling and religious education subverts the *rights of children*. Fourth, that these matters are to be resolved by reference to the '*parent-child-state axis*' which remains to be clarified by a proper understanding of moral obligations and permissions. And finally, that this understanding will be provided by a system of *universal rights*.

At this point I wish to remind the reader of the fact that this is an example, now bridging the practical and the theoretical, of the ambition, and, as has just been seen, of the grim and threatening determination, to reduce the range of moral categories to a unitary form; that of legally enforceable rights. The theoretical aspect I will turn to in a moment, but notice first that these moral imperialists are not content to pursue exclusive control of conceptual space and the associated moral language; they also want to implement ideological mastery in the real world of human relationships using the force of the state to do so.

Promotional announcements of forthcoming films used to be accompanied by the slogan 'coming soon to a cinema near you'. Adapting this I might say 'Look out for a unitary moral system and its socio-political implementation for it will be coming soon to a community near you.' I realise that this has all of the brevity and literary style of a Stalinist policy directive, but that very association may serve to imprint the warning it carries.

To this point I have been discussing the threat to traditional values posed by various forms of cultural imperialism, the last of which has arisen within ethics itself. Before saying something about the future let me say more about the structure of ethics since this will help us to see where we are intellectually, what may be expected, and what I think should be aimed for.

The English terms 'ethics' and 'ethical' and their equivalents in other European languages deriving from the Latin '*ethice*' and from the Greek '*Ethikos*', are used in a variety of ways:

To refer

1. to professional standards of conduct (as in 'legal ethics');
2. to a person's general moral position (as in 'Bush's ethical perspective');
3. to general conduct or values (as in 'contemporary European ethics');
4. to the systematic treatment of moral aspects of the situation (as in 'let's take stock of the ethical dimension of this');
5. to the academic study of moral issues (as in 'ethical theory').

This diversity can be understood in terms of a three level distinction between

I. *Ordinary moral thinking*: judgements that such and such is good/bad; right/wrong; virtuous/vicious; and so on.
II. *Moral theories*: systematic efforts to justify ordinary moral thinking.
III.*Metaethical theories*: philosophical accounts of the status of (i) ordinary moral thinking, and (ii) moral theories.

The theoretical debates about subjectivism vs. objectivism, relativism vs. realism, and so on, occur at the third philosophical level, though something of them features, or is presupposed, in abstract talk about 'ethics' engaged in by non-philosophers. Here I am not concerned with metaethics, in part because it is the most theoretical branch of ethics and it is hard to enter debates without already being familiar with the often technical terms in which they are now framed. I will just report that whereas fifty years ago most professional philosophers were drawn to versions of subjectivism, today most favour certain forms of objectivism, or at least cognitivism. That is to say they would agree that even if there are no moral 'objects' (such as free floating values) there is at least moral knowledge; and that is a rejection of the earlier orthodoxy that moral claims are simply expressions of attitudes of favouring or disfavouring things.

Turning then to moral theories these can be best be understood, and the differences between them described in terms of the issue of what aspect of action is morally primary. We may distinguish between an agent, his character, motives, and intentions, and an action itself, the thing done, and between both of these and the result or consequence of the action. Ultimately any developed moral theory will have something to say about each of these elements when it comes to making a moral evaluation, but generally a moral theory will give priority to the assessment of one of the three elements: agent, act and outcome, and then explain the value of the other elements secondarily.

So if one thinks that what matters ultimately is the good or bad resulting from an agent's actions then one will judge the action by reference to these consequences. If, however, one holds that what matters first and foremost is the doing or refraining from the doing of certain kinds of actions, say being charitable or not being unfaithful, then an agent and an outcome will be judged in terms of their relationship to these requirements and prohibitions. Finally, if one takes the view that what is of ultimate value are the character, motive and intentions of the agent then the moral value of what is done and of what results will derive from these features.

These three accounts of the locus or centre of moral value correspond to the three main forms of moral theory presented, criticised and defended today among moral philosophers and among Christian theologians influenced by moral philosophy, namely utilitarian, deontological, and virtue-centred ethical theories. Rights-based approaches, such as were invoked (controversially) by the critics of parental choice with regard to children's schooling and religious education, are generally applications of either utilitarianism or deontology.

Speaking sociologically, public discourse about ethics tends to be a bit of a mix, but the dominant element is utilitarian in one form or another. Moral theologians at least in the West tend to follow in the wake of philosophical fashions, though generally catching up with them after they have fallen out of favour among philosophers themselves. For example, the 'situation ethics' of Joseph Fletcher, and the 'proportionalism' of Richard McCormick represent the adoption within moral theology of approaches originating in moral philosophy. Little surprise then that two decades after the revival of virtue ethics in philosophy it became quite the fashion in moral theology, in which connection see for example writings by Stanley Hauerwas and Jean Porter.

One answer, therefore, to the question what will be the future trends in Christian Ethics in Europe? (if one means by this Christian ethics in Western Europe) is that it will be a Christianised, or at least theologised version of what was fashionable among secular moral philosophers in the preceding period; and since hedonistic utilitarianism has made a revival among philosophers so too will it became more prominent again among moral theologians.

If, however, one is interested in the question of what direction Christian ethics *ought* to take in the future then I would want to make three points. First, in identifying the three approaches – utilitarianism, deontology and virtue theory – I used the device of seeking evaluative priority between motive, act and outcome, but one may, Aquinas did, and I believe one should, reject the idea of there being a single fundamental site of value. To seek for such is, I think, another instance of the craving to simplify, reduce and unify. Instead we should recognise that all three elements, and perhaps others besides, are integral to ethical value.

Second, I think it would be a mistake to try to develop some kind of pure divine command, or theological theory to the effect that the good is what God commands because, and *only because*, he commands it. That position is vulnerable to the challenge presented in Plato's *Euthyphro* dialogue to the effect that the purported goodness of the gods is measured by whether what they command is indeed pious and good.

Third, however, I do believe that there is an ineliminably theological, or at any rate religious dimension to any Christian understanding of conduct, but this enters in not with the theory of ethics but with the account of the meaning and purpose of life, its aim and its completion. Ethics, strictly speaking, is a negative science or art. It tells you what you may not do, what you may not intentionally aim to bring about, and what you may not become as a person. By itself, however, it lacks positive direction. Knowing what not to do is insufficient to know how to shape one's life and to what end to direct it. This, however, is precisely what the Christian Gospel and its implementation in the lives of the saints provide us with: a direction and examples of how to orient oneself and move towards that *telos*.

So in a sense the proper future trend in Christian ethics in Europe should be towards the proper Christian future: to love, to know and to serve God, and for his sake to love and to serve others. In the abstract the structure of this is simple enough, but in the concrete it is hard to live out. Why that should be so is something that the Christian understanding also addresses, namely the falleness of human kind, and for which it promises the remedy of supernatural grace. These last matters were once items of common knowledge among literate people but now they have to be reported and explained even to college and university graduates, such is the condition of Christian culture in Europe.

The Vienna statement spoke of the influence of Eastern and Western Churches in 'the formation of distinctive cultures on the European continent and in other parts of the world'. This raises the question of whether in the contest with secularism the Catholic and Orthodox Churches should now prepare to widen the scope of their discussions to bring in Christians from beyond Europe. In due course that will probably happen, but for now the world can watch with interest to see where this new dialogue goes to next.

Section V

Beauty, art and education

21.

Art and vocation

On Easter Sunday 1999 Pope John Paul II addressed a *Letter to Artists*. It begins with a notion of productive creativity broader than that associated with the idea of the fine arts, literature and music; next it distinguishes this from the narrower aesthetic conception; but then it reconnects them through the idea that artists, like others, disclose their own being ... what they are and how they are what they are' through their activity. The Pope wrote:

Not all are called to be artists in the specific sense of the term. Yet, as Genesis has it, all men and women are entrusted with the task of crafting their own life: in a certain sense, they are to make of it a work of art, a masterpiece.

It is important to recognize the distinction, but also the connection, between these two aspects of human activity. The distinction is clear. It is one thing for human beings to be the authors of their own acts, with responsibility for their moral value; it is another to be an artist, able, that is, to respond to the demands of art and faithfully to accept art's specific dictates. This is what makes the artist capable of producing objects, but it says nothing as yet of his moral character. We are speaking not of moulding oneself, of forming one's own personality, but simply of actualizing one's productive capacities, giving aesthetic form to ideas conceived in the mind.

The distinction between the moral and artistic aspects is fundamental, but no less important is the connection between them. Each conditions the other in a profound way.

Before discussing some of his themes it is worth noting than in addressing artists (in the aesthetic sense) the author was engaging in a kind of reflexive act, for he himself, was an artist. From his teenage years in the period leading up to the Second World War, Karol Wojtyla was involved in theatrical performances in Wadowice; and once at the Jagiellonian University in Krakow he joined Studio 38, an experimental theatre group founded and directed by Tadeusz Kudlinski. During that period he wrote the play *Our God's Brother*, and later *The Jeweller's Shop* both of which were subsequently made into films. Between 1946 and 1979 he also wrote and published poetry under the pseudonym Andrzej Jawien. In one of these works he writes:

> The stuff or ordinary days in me
> is continuously transformed,
> seeking an outlet like a river
> weighed to the bottom by its own weight

and elsewhere human creativity is related to river imagery which now serves another purpose

> Fear not. Man's daily deeds have a wide span,
> a strait riverbed can't imprison them long.
> Fear not. For centuries they all stand in Him,
> and you look at Him now
> through the even knocking of hammers.

These and other poems from the 1940s to the 1970s were gathered and translated by Jerzy Peterkiewicz, himself a poet and novelist, and published as *Collected Poems of Karol Wojtyla* (1985). They show the poet to be focused on a single complex theme: the condition of human beings throughout time seeking, individually and socially, salvation from ignorance, fear, oppression, corruption and death. Repeatedly the poet calls for faith, wisdom, courage and strength, and offers reminders of them from everyday life. The philosophical conception of human beings was worked out in academic writings such as *The Acting Person* (1979). As that title suggests the human essence is taken to consist in embodied agency. Not only is human nature most perfectly disclosed in action, but it is through what one does that one 'creates oneself' as an individual. And when this process is informed by the recognition of values and directed by grace we are drawn towards the perfection of humanity revealed in Christ.

> Sometimes it happens in conversation:
> we stand facing truth and lack the words,
> have no gesture, no sign;
> and yet – we feel – no word, no gesture or sign
> could convey the whole image
> that we must enter alone and face, like Jacob.
> This isn't the mere wrestling with images
> Carried in our thoughts;
> We fight with the likeness of all things
> That inwardly constitute man.
> But when we act can our deeds surrender
> the ultimate truths we presume to ponder?

This self-exploration informs the *Letter to Artists*. It a characteristic blend of philosophical, aesthetic and theological reminders of the condition and orientation of incarnate human persons. We are made for God but we have to find our way to Him, and that involves aiming ourselves toward a goal. The notion of an end occurs twice here: first, as a *destination* or terminus; but second, as a *state* or condition to which, with God's grace, we have to bring ourselves. This latter is the business of self-realisation: the process of becoming fully and actually what, in part and in potentiality, we already are.

Herein enter both ethics and art. The Pope is right to distinguish but not to sever them. Kant believed that thought and experience divide into three categories: the *speculative*, the *practical*, and the *aesthetic* (hence the three great *Critiques* of 'pure' and of 'practical' reason, and of 'judgement'). In the Thomistic tradition, however, the category of the practical subsumes both the moral and aesthetic since it views the latter as primarily a matter of activity – as Thomas Aquinas observes: 'In art, the mind is directed to some specific aim, while in morality it is directed to an aim shared by all human life' (*Summa Theologiae*, Ia, IIae, q. a. ad). To be sure, there is the aesthetic as *experienced* beauty – disinterested contemplation of form for its own sake. But this most commonly arises from making and from reviewing what one, or others have made. For this reason the aesthetic of nature properly suggests the idea of a maker of nature.

That is not yet a proof, for it could be that the appearance of aesthetic order in the natural world is an illusion. For example, the apparent composition in the forms of living things; the dramatic opposition between the heights reaching toward the burning light, and the depths plunging into the chilling dark, could just be projections onto an aesthetically blank world. The possibility of a persuasive design argument remains, however, if, as I have claimed, the idea of beauty is internally related to that of aesthetic design; and if, as I would also maintain, the appearances of natural beauty, recorded by people of different cultures, places, and times, are as they indeed appear, namely aspects of the world. One might add, 'of the world *as experienced*,' for as St Thomas also observes 'beauty complements good by subordinating it to the cognitive powers ... beauty is that, the very perception of which is pleasing'.

In distinguishing ethics and art, the Pope may also have had in mind two opposing errors into which one may fall, having correctly recognised the truth that there are important connections between the moral and the aesthetic; namely those of aestheticising the moral, and of moralising the aesthetic. We may speak rhetorically of the 'beauty' of good character, and of the 'artistry' of a well-designed policy; but it is as easy to speak of the 'drama' of degeneracy and of the 'thrilling anticipation' of moral tragedy. Certainly much aestheticising has been directed upon these latter. The 'decadents' sought to make a point about how art could be severed from morality by showing that it could serve the interests of decline as well as of improvement. Wilde's *Portrait of Dorian Gray* is a rather contrived effort in this direction, as are Aubrey Beardsley's flat and lifeless illustrations for Wilde's *Salome*. The fact that, it seems, both men turned to the Church as they approached death says something about their souls but does nothing to enhance the status of these works. It does, though, encourage the thought that had things been otherwise in their lives, and in the surrounding culture, then they might have developed their talents in artistically and aesthetically more profound ways.

Notice, by the way, that the decadents sought both to give aesthetic celebration to evil, and to elevate art to a moral calling. In this latter regard 'art' has to be understood as artistry, that is as a set of skills for literary or graphic composition, delineation and expression. While there is much to be said for the cultivation of these skills, as of any that have the potential to realise fundamental human goods, the decadents erred twice in seeing themselves as noble spirits: first, because the values in whose service their artistry was deployed were negatives, that is disvalues; but second, and less obviously, because they encouraged the assumption that others of good intent have also made, that artistry is not as such neutral, that it is, like moral virtue, intrinsically directed toward nonaesthetic goods. But this is what Plato exposed in the *Republic*: a skill (*techne*) is precisely neutral as between opposing ends. He who in virtue of knowing medicine can alleviate suffering and effect a cure, can, by the same knowledge, bring pain and death. Likewise, artistry may be technically competent or incompetent, but when competent – even excellent – it can still be used badly. Not all art is good in either the technical or in the external evaluative senses.

Yet there is at least an analogy of excellence between artistry and moral character, and one might hope that as an artist develops her skills, so she might want to conjoin them with an equal depth of informed feeling about the human condition. As and when that occurs, one might expect the artist to look around for a *logos* – an account of the deepest meaning of this condition. And since we may assume that the deepest and truest account of it is that afforded by Catholic anthropology, so we may hope that the sincere artist will be drawn to this and be inspired by it.

So we come to religious art. John Paul's phenomenological orientation shows itself in his observation that 'In song, faith is *experienced* as vibrant joy, love and confident expectation of the saving intervention of God' (my emphasis). This is true for those of faith (and of fair ear and voice); but what of those who hear the glories of a sung Mass, say, but lack faith? Can art be a route to God? Of course, psychologically it may indeed be an occasion of conversion; and we saw earlier that there might be an argument from the experience of beauty to the idea of an author of it. But the first is a matter of empirical contingency (strictly, anything may be an *occasion* of anything else); and the second concerned the aesthetics of nature. What I have in mind now is the different possibility that the experience of religious art might provide rational grounds for coming to a religious conclusion.

How might this be? After all, is not the implication of my earlier comments that artistry can serve *any* end, and so we must distinguish what is said from how well it is expressed? If so, then however beautifully the Creed is scored and rendered, its setting and performance offer no testament to its truth. But here a new distinction has emerged. The first was that between *skill* and *end*; now we have shifted to one between *form* and *content*. Indeed, bad things may be beautifully said, and true words ill-delivered. But in these cases we have a sense that the same things might be said differently, and aesthetically better or worse. In other words we are assuming that the form and the content are separable, but supposing that in some cases they are not.

Consider a facial expression that communicates a certain attitude of its bearer. One may be able to say what that attitude is, independently of the expression; but equally one may not. One may only be able to say to someone else 'she looked at me in that special kindly way of hers – you know *the way* I mean.' Here 'look' and 'attitude' are not separable: the facial expression is the moment of kindness. See it and you register the state. Put another way, it is the ground of one's conviction that kindness is there, and of one's being comforted by it.

Now suppose that one hears an inspired rendering of Palestrina's *Missa Papae Marcelli* or Tallis's *Spem in alium* and it seems transcendent; a movement away from here into another place; not a spatial location but a place whose dimensions are religious; one shaped by creation, grace, judgment, and loving sacrifice. Might one not say to another 'I felt transported and made present before this – you know *the way* I mean.' Of course a hearer may not; but that no more shows that one's experience was not veridical than does the fact that in the case of kindness someone else may not recognise that experience either. Here we see what a severe criticism it is of religious art (and ipso facto of such artists) to say that it is (and hence that they are) 'merely illustrative'. Great religious art does not *illustrate* the religious, it is animated by and expresses it; just as a facial gesture may be animated by and express kindness. That is the religious challenge to artists: to be living forms of the Living Word (*logos*).

22.

On religious architecture

In the year of the millennium, the Liturgy Committee of the US Conference of Catholic Bishops published a document entitled *Built of Living Stones: Art, Architecture, and Worship* (2000). This was intended to replace an earlier statement somewhat prosaically, and datedly, entitled *Environment and Art in Catholic Worship* (1978). That earlier document had been the subject of considerable and long-lasting controversy especially around issues of liturgy and of the presumed authority of its declarations.

It was in part to end these that the new statement was produced, though it has also had something of a mixed reception and has like its predecessor has attracted criticism from those who see it failing to acknowledge established liturgical norms. These matters are not my concern, rather I am interested in a broader, deeper and prior issue.

The stated purpose of *Built of Living Stones* is 'to assist the faithful involved in the building or renovation of churches, chapels, and oratories of the Latin Church in the United States', but quite properly it addresses general issues about the nature and role of religious buildings and offers as its first chapter 'a theological reflection' on *The Living Church*. An important conceptual element of that is the following on 'The Church Building':

Just as the term Church refers to the living temple, God's People, the term church also has been used to describe 'the building in which the Christian community gathers to hear the word of God, to pray together, to receive the sacraments, and celebrate the eucharist.' That building is both the house of God on earth (*domus Dei*) and a house fit for the prayers of the saints (*domus ecclesiae*). Such a house of prayer must be expressive of the presence of God and suited for the celebration of the sacrifice of Christ, as well as reflective of the community that celebrates there.

While this statement is theologically unexceptionable it raises certain philosophical questions that are not themselves addressed: principally, that of how a building can express the presence of God, or more broadly how architecture can be religious – not in the sense of having that function but of embodying or expressing religious realities. Perhaps it was not for the authors of the text to engage these questions but they are important, particularly in a period when religious sensibilities, let alone practice, are reduced, and when people look with uncertainty to see what if any evidence there is or could be of the existence of God. So let me begin to address these questions by providing a philosophical reflection on the idea of religious architecture.

It is a fact of human experience that interior spaces can induce feelings of quietness, reflective calm, and natural piety. It is also the case that the massing of volumes upwards may create a sense of transcendence, as if suggesting the possibility that, like the stones themselves, the viewer can rise above the earth on which he stands. These responses are often difficult to characterise and generally they cannot be made precise, nonetheless they are undeniable. If the experience of space and solid forms did not prompt them then architecture, as contrasted with mere building, would not exist and, *a fortiori*, religious architecture would be impossible.

The possibility of religious or 'spiritual' architecture depends on the fact that human beings respond in certain ways to physical forms. What more can be said about this? One approach would be to look for a materialistic-evolutionary explanation. In recent years there has been an increasing interest in environmental aesthetics, and in particular in the aesthetic experience of natural environments such as mountains and valleys, and moors and woodlands. One school of thought about our experiences of these attempts to explain particular preferences and affinities – for example, for landscapes that combine open vistas with outcrops of rock and clusters of shrubs and trees – in terms of our natural history as one time hunter-gatherers.

For our remote ancestors such environments offered opportunities to seek and to hide from prey. Those who were alert to and took advantage of these landscape features enjoyed competitive success in the struggle for survival. Consequently they had greater numbers of surviving offspring possessed of the same responsiveness to seek-and-hide environments. As descendants of such populations we retain a sensitivity that is triggered by similar landscapes, giving rise to feelings of familiarity and pleasure. Likewise one might try to connect the experience of architectural forms to some more primitive and ancient association with places of significance to our primordial ancestors, such as caves and crevices.

Without denying the possibility that present experiences have some link to practical necessities of the long-distant past, it is important to understand why such explanations are partial – at best. Suppose we asked, by analogy, why portraits tend to show the sitter face on, or again why still-life paintings often depict fruit. Someone might reply that for our ancestors it was important to see the expression in the eyes of others in order to tell whether they were friend or foe. Similarly there is a long human history of fruit-gathering so the sight of this now evokes feelings of familiarity and pleasure. While these claims may be true, all they serve to explain are very general features of our interests, and why our attention may be caught by this or that.

Such answers do not explain why pleasure is taken in,

and value is attached to, one or other genre of representation of faces or of fruit; or why, critically, some paintings of either subjects are judged better than others. So with architecture. A natural disposition to enclosed spaces and high structures may derive from ancestral associations with caves and mountains, but at most this establishes a very broad area within which the aesthetics of architecture operates. It does not begin to explain the relative merit of different traditions, classical, Romanesque, Gothic, baroque and so on, let alone the quality of individual buildings. Nor does it explain how a structure or part of it could embody or express particular religious or spiritual ideas and feelings.

What needs adding is the fact that wood, stone and glass, like paper, canvas and paint, may be used as media for the communication of experiences and ideas. Architecture is a form of embodied meaning. Sometimes people speak of the 'language of architecture', but that may be misleading if it suggests that buildings are linguistically-structured like essays or stories, made up of the equivalent of sentences, themselves composed out of elements corresponding to words. Nonetheless it is appropriate to think of buildings as vessels of meaning, or as bearing a significance, and in this way it is proper to speak of 'reading' or interpreting a building: working out the meaning of the parts and of the whole.

Earlier I criticised the kind of reductionism that attempts to reduce the significance of aesthetic experience to a speculated origin in ancestral needs and interests. Now I wish to criticise reductionism of a different kind. The first was proposed by ethnologists and social anthropologists, the second is the work of philosophers. This is the empiricist view that experience is no more than the impact of the physical environment upon the sense organs. Empiricism is prepared to allow that our thoughts about the world are more complex than immediate impressions of colour, sound, touch, odour and taste, but its advocates insist that all genuine content must somehow be traceable back or reducible to immediate sense-impressions.

If that were so then the prospects for experiences of religious, spiritual or other meaning would be nil, and we would have to conclude (as some do) that all talk of 'experiential understanding' is incoherent. At most, aesthetics could consist in pleasurable experiences accompanying certain sensations, like the ease felt sitting quietly with one's face to the sun, or the satisfaction at standing and stretching. But as anyone well knows who reflects on their experience of designed forms and spaces, or who reads art or architectural descriptions, aesthetic experience goes far beyond the pleasures of mere sense and constitutes a rich and rewarding mode of understanding. It is one thing to be rooted in sensation, quite another to be confined to it.

To make sense of the idea that art and architecture can be vehicles of spiritual understanding, we need a better account of experience. Part of the inspiration for empiricism is that in perception the senses are affected by the environment. It is a mistake, however, to conclude that perceiving is reducible to sensation. Seeing is a discriminating activity by intelligent, interpretative beings. To see a face or an apple is not to infer them from sensations, it is to encounter real objects directly, whose nature and significance are understood on the basis of a broad and shared understanding of the world. Perception may depend upon sensation as its material basis, but it transcends this and belongs to the order of understanding.

The experience of art and architecture involves intellectual, emotional and evaluative capacities working together to make sense of what is seen and moved through. Similarly, in conceiving a drawing or a building, the artist or architect seeks to embody his or her own understanding of things as derived from prior experience and reflection. In this way pigment and paper, stone and glass are taken up into a medium of expression, and are thereby transformed into bearers of meaning. The resulting expressive and symbolic orders may then serve to represent aspects of mundane and transcendent realities. Art and architecture cannot embody knowledge we do not have, but importantly they can contribute to the development of understanding

The experience of architecture involves intellectual, emotional and evaluative capacities working together to make sense of what is seen and moved through. Similarly, in designing a building an architect seeks to embody his or own understanding of things as derived from prior experience and reflection. In this way stone and glass, wood and metal, are taken up into a medium of expression and transformed into bearers of religious and other meanings. The resulting symbolic order may then serve to represent aspects of mundane and transcendent reality. Religious architecture cannot convey knowledge we do not possess. It is not a substitute for faith; but it can give tangible expression to the inklings of the soul and to the theology of the Church. Thus it can and it should be part of the effort to know, to love and to serve God.

23.

Religious art and religious education

One of the purposes of religious education, understood as a kind of formation of character, mind and imagination, is to enable a recipient of it to develop a religious outlook. Developing such an outlook involves, among other things, coming to appreciate various phenomena for their religious significance and value. It is an important question for formal teaching, but also for informal education and personal development how such an outlook might be acquired and cultivated. It is not possible to explore these issues fully here but I do want to discuss the place of art in achieving a religious outlook. In particular I want to consider how looking at paintings can serve the need to develop relevant sensitivities by which one may be receptive to religious realities and respond appropriately to them. Though once familiar this subject has been somewhat neglected in recent times, perhaps due in part to the poverty of contemporary religious art.

For various reasons not least the secularisation of education and culture, and the corresponding decline in the temporal power and authority of the Church, painters turned from depicting religious themes and increasingly became preoccupied with the activity of painting itself. Thus if one wishes to study religious art of a consistently high standard it is profitable to look back to the work of earlier ages. In saying this I do not mean to suggest that there is no good contemporary religious art, only that there is precious little.

Before dealing with religious art as such, however, it is worth remarking that other kinds of aesthetic experience may contribute to the development of a religious outlook. Reflection on beauty as realised in nature and in works of art may have a part to play, whether or not the objects in question are obviously religious. Just as the experience of standing in a landscape may occasion a sense of the contingency of the world and its dependence on a sustaining cause, so contemplating Cézanne's views on Mont Sainte-Victoire may induce a similar response. Indeed, given the artist's ability to focus on certain aspects of a scene and to highlight them, it may be expected that often the aesthetic experience is clearer and more sharply defined in response to a work of art than when felt as a vague reaction to the grandeur of nature.

Be this as it may, there is a further point to looking at paintings created as religious works. One way in which such pictures serve our purpose is obvious, namely when art is employed in a purely illustrative role. Following the Christianisation of the Roman empire the need to build places of worship led in turn to debate about their decoration. The conclusion of this, in the Latin West, was signalled by Pope Gregory the Great when he noted that 'painting can do for the illiterate what writing does for those who can read' i.e. represent biblical episodes and illustrate Christian doctrines. This notion of the role of art received a touching echo nine hundred years later when François Villon wrote of his devout and God-fearing mother:

> I am a woman, poor and old,
> I can neither read nor spell.
> At Mass in church, here, I behold,
> A painted Heaven, with harps: a Hell,
> Where the damned are boiled, as well.
> One gives me joy: one strikes me cold,
> Grant me the joy, Great Goddess,
> On whom all sinners must rely,
> Fill me with faith and no slackness.
> In this faith let me live and die.

Clearly this conception of the function of painting as representation is limited though it has its place and a corresponding use of art in religious education suggests itself. At one stage little else may be possible and it may be useful later to return to finely-rendered representations of this kind to enrich the imagination, or to prompt reflection on the subjects depicted. Whatever its merits, however, the employment of religious art as narrative is only a beginning; for what is to be aimed at is the recovery of the artist's vision. We have to try to capture for ourselves and for others the imaginative experience as it is embodied in the work. Certainly a religious piece that is lacking in the appropriate feelings may yet serve the purpose of relating events, but the real instrumental value of works infused with religious sentiment is that they reveal, even to the literate, truths that words cannot convey.

In the developed world human consciousness has been shaped by empirical and theoretical discourses constructed according to certain norms of rational enquiry. The benefits of these ways of thinking are evident; its disadvantages are less easily observed, partly because the style of living that results from according primacy to empirical and intellectual modes draws attention away from the realm of intuition and imagination. The truth, however, is that intellectual cognition is a coarse net with which to try to catch all that is real and of importance; and the words we use to try to describe completely the reality that confronts us are often poor tools for such a task. Even quite ordinary experience involves bringing objects under some description, and this requires that one go beyond what is immediately present to the senses. Perception and the thoughts it prompts are always informed, and as the quantity and variety of one's experience increases so the range of descriptions grows, and with them the scope for ever richer and more discriminating interpretations and evaluations. Just as a line on a piece of paper is no longer seen simply as a configuration, or as a piece of writing, or as a signature, but is perceived to exhibit authority and perhaps concern; so a state of affairs admits of increasingly sensitive perceptions: a man extends his hand, and in so doing draws another closer, thereby showing his forgiveness, and in the circumstances this demonstrates his limitless and unqualified love.

It is for this kind of revelatory description that one turns to great artists, and where their subjects are religious one hopes to benefit from their hard-won insights. 'Insights' because they have ways of seeing the significance in things beyond what is immediately present; 'hard-won' because such inspired perception does not come easily or at little cost; it has to be worked at by looking in the hope, vain though it is, of exhausting the depth of meaning. Religious sensitivity consists in a capacity to discover and interpret the significance of certain episodes. Adopting the language of faculties of mind, *intuition* and *imagination* are the mental powers relevant to discovering religious meaning. Artists and visionaries possess these capacities to a high degree and it is they therefore who are best able to discern the transcendent truth manifest in a situation or state of affairs. Ideally they are also able to translate this vision into some form that makes it accessible to the rest of us who would otherwise remain insensitive to its real value. A work of art is thus a response to what is significant in its subject, and by looking at such works one may come to share the truth the artist discovers there.

In all of this the challenge to the artist is both aesthetic and theological. If the work he or she produces is to be good art it must realise certain aesthetic values. For example, the form must be appropriate to its content and the whole must achieve a sense of completeness and independence; but for it to be properly religious it must express something of the truth about God, his creation and his will. As I noted, there is a place for the merely illustrative work, but if one hopes to develop in oneself and in others a genuinely religious sensitivity it is essential that one looks to works that embody the product of a good deal of religious thought and feeling. Having developed a personal response to religious truth the creators of such art manage to instil some aspect of it into a work where it remains to be recovered by whoever has the ability to do so.

Given this brief account of how the study of art may be relevant to religious education it may be useful to illustrate something of what is at issue by reference to a few well-known examples. Consider first Piero della Francesca's *The Baptism of Christ*. In the foreground and beneath the dove of the Holy Spirit stands Christ, hands joined in prayer, while John the Baptist reaches up to pour water from a dish over his head. To Christ's right, and behind a tree, stand a group of angelic figures curiously uninvolved in the event; while in the background a man prepares himself to be immersed in the waters of the Jordan. Such are the bare facts of the episode. Jesus has come to be baptised like many before him and John meets his request. The significance of the event, of course, lies deeper than this matter of fact description reveals. John's message is for the people to 'Prepare the way of the Lord' for 'all flesh shall see the salvation of God'. Baptism by water represents repentance at past sins and renewal in anticipation of the coming of the Messiah. Yet when Christ, the Promised One, does arrive he too asks to be baptised. John protests that it is not fitting and that he John should be baptised by Jesus. Yet, in obedience to the command 'Let it be so for now' he accedes and performs the ceremony. As he does so the dove descends upon Christ and the words are heard 'This is my beloved Son with whom I am well pleased' at which point John's mission is completed for the identity of the Messiah, of whom John was the forerunner, has been revealed.

What does Piero make of this important occasion? First one needs to notice that John has one leg bent backwards as he reaches up to baptise Jesus. By this device one senses something of the greater stature of the latter, and this impression is made more acute by the solidity of Christ, the only figure to stand face on to the viewer. But compositionally and metaphorically Jesus is at the very centre of the scene, and it is on him that we are invited to focus and to concentrate – the further implied invitation being to follow him as disciples. There is, as it were, a double message: I need you; and you need me. Second, one is struck by the faces of the participants. None seems particularly animated and there is a feeling of stillness, as if a silence has settled while John baptises his Lord and master. All present have become oblivious to what else is going around them and are taken up by the mystical atmosphere in which they seem to be aware of some transcendent, perhaps timeless, reality lying beyond but indicated by the events of this world. One could write at length about this powerful religious work but all I wish to convey are possibilities for reflection on great religious art. For in this way one may come to share in the artist's vision, and thereby increase one's understanding of the subjects he represents. Looking at paintings can serve to bring to life aspects of religious truth that previously were unthought of; and thereby one's faith may be enriched.

A quite different though no less impressive work is Giovanni Bellini's portrayal of *The Agony in the Garden*. Here four men are grouped in the foreground: three sleeping Apostles (Peter, James and John), and on the right of the picture raised on a rock and with his back to the viewer is the praying figure of Christ. Meanwhile there approaches in the distance along the road that cuts across the background, a crowd of figures among whom is Judas who we know will betray his master with a kiss. Once again a feeling of stillness pervades the scene but this time the focus of events is not a cause for joy but rather an occasion for sorrow. In the sky above and to the right of Jesus stands an angel his arms outstretched and with a chalice in his hands. This reminds us of the impending sacrifice by which Christ will make good the debt owing to God by man who has broken the covenant first made with Abraham and thereafter renewed and breached in consequence of human sin. A further reminder of the impending trial and crucifixion is provided by the thorn-like fencing that encloses the garden where Jesus awaits his betrayer. Turning to the Apostles we see them fast asleep and unable to comfort their Lord in his agony. In them also one may see a reflection of one's own lack of constancy in the practice of prayer and of faith more generally.

It is interesting to compare this work with another of the same subject by an exact contemporary, viz. Andrea Mantegna. The latter painting is more ornate: the whole scene being animated by the swirling lines of stratification of the surrounding rocks, by the grand scale of the land-scape, and by the equally magnificent architecture of the old city of Jerusalem as Mantegna represents it. Further-more, whereas Bellini has a solitary angel, in Mantegna's composition the number has increased to a host of five. It is clear that he has been preoccupied with the new tech-niques of painting, particularly linear perspective within the landscape and foreshortening of the human figure, and that he is proudly keen to put his knowledge and skill to maximum effect in a dramatic and elaborate master-piece. But if this work is more painterly in those respects it is also more indulgent and a good deal of the religious feeling that infuses Bellini's work is absent. While the latter's almost empty sky and landscape heightens the sense of Christ's isolation, and of the existential moment of choice and acceptance of death, the activity of Mantegna's work only serves to obliterate this central aspect of the occasion.

Again it would be possible to pursue the themes almost without limit but my aim has only been to illustrate how attention to art can have a place in the development of a religious sensibility and in the discernment of religious truths. If religious education is to be effective it must touch the whole personality of the student. It must engage and appeal to affective faculties as much as to the intellect and the imagination. History and doctrine are inelim-inable elements of such an education, but the development of religious feeling and an appreciation of the values at which it aims are also required if the former beliefs are to constitute a living faith.

My concern has been to trace one way in which a religious outlook might be developed, and this suggests various practical steps that could be taken to incorporate these conclusions in the work of the religious educator – including the self-educator. Within the context of schooling, whatever the pressures of time with access to the internet, it is easier today than in the past to acquire examples of good religious art for children to study in the phenomenological interpretative manner I have illustrated. Instructing them in appreciation, as well as encouraging them to make efforts to translate their own moral and religious understandings into pictorial form, is an activity that can hardly fail to be of value to the teacher as well to the pupil.

24.

On Catholic schools

Not all education takes the form of schooling or even of formal instruction. It is important to remember this, since we live in a period in which basic human activities have been socially organised, institutionalised, politically governed and legally regulated. Some of these developments were inevitable as social and economic life became more complex, and some aspects of them are certainly beneficial. At the same time, however, these organisational and regulatory tendencies give rise to two dangers. On the one hand that individuals neglect their own responsibilities in such matters, perhaps even forgetting that they have such responsibilities; and on the other that society, in the form of politicians and policy advocates, imposes its views and values against the interests of individuals and groups. Here I am concerned with such matters as they arise in connection with Catholic education.

The place of religion in education is an issue apt for dispute. It could hardly be otherwise given that, unlike arithmetic or geography, religion itself is an essentially contentious subject. But that is in part because of the depth and importance of the matters it deals with, nothing less than the meaning of life, death and all existence. It needs to be allowed, therefore, that this is an area in which agreement is not likely to be easily reached or long maintained. Nonetheless, and in response to recent challenges voiced in the press and media, I believe that the case can

be made for state support of Catholic schools on philosophical, educational and political grounds.

The complaints against state support for Catholic
schools (and a parallel case might be made against schools
of other faiths and denominations) is, first, that they are
socially divisive, demanding special funding and encouraging religious intolerance; and, second, that they are
educationally suspect: devoting time to religious instruction and worship at the expense of other parts of the
curriculum and practising indoctrination rather than
education.

The claim of social divisiveness needs some analysis. If
it simply amounts to the idea that if some children attend
schools of type A and others attend schools of types B or C
then not all members of society will have shared the same
sort of education, it is evidently trivial. In this sense social
division is implied by the truth that no two schools (or two
persons) are identical. Of course opponents have something more substantial in mind, but without clear evidence
of detrimental effects on social cohesion resulting directly
from the existence of such schools there is no reason to
think that diversity is intrinsically divisive in some
substantial sense. Indeed, one might suppose that diversity within a society may enrich it.

It will be replied, however, that there is evidence of the
bad effect of separate schooling provided most immediately by the history of sectarian division in Northern
Ireland, where, as in mainland Britain, Roman Catholics
have their own schools within the state maintained sector.
Clearly Ulster remains in a state of tragic disunity and the
sharp divide between those of loyalist and republican
commitments is associated with Protestant and Catholic
allegiance. It is equally clear, however, that the policy of
separate schooling is an expression and not the cause of
these divisions. These days the most violent exchanges in
Ulster are in fact between rival loyalist groups whose
differences have no religious aspect.

Community divisions and violence in Northern Ireland,

and their shadows on this side of the Irish Sea, are a political problem not a religious one, and they do not make the
case for withdrawing support for denominational schools.
Indeed, if there is any place to look for hope in these parts
it is to the efforts of teachers and religious leaders within
the different communities to show through education and
example that the political differences between them, let
alone violence, cannot be justified by different religious
attachments.

It may be replied that religion is still a mark of the basic
divisions and that separate schooling sustains these
distinctions. What that response reveals, however, is that
the real target of the objection is not denominational
schools but the very existence of different religious
communities. It is a mistake to suppose that if all
members of society shared the same beliefs there would be
no divisions between them; but even if such a uniformity
of view could secure this it would surely be an abuse of the
education system to use it to eliminate diversity of fundamental beliefs and practices. To engage in this would be to
practice precisely that vice of which advocates of religious
schools stand accused, namely, failing to respect the
autonomy of those in their charge by indoctrinating them
into a single system of belief.

Government derives its authority from the whole people
whose views it is obliged to respect. It is a notoriously
difficult question to say what the bounds of state authority
may be, but it is a mark of Western politics to acknowledge
that there are limits, and that without very good reason
the state may not act contrary to a citizen's deeply held
wish for his own good and that of his family. Recognition
that the education of one's children is in this category of
protected entitlement is made by the Human Rights
declarations of the United Nations and the European
Convention for the Protection of Human Rights. Acknowledgement of the same rights of parents to choose schools
for their children is implicit in the conscience clauses of
current British education legislation. Thus any move to

eliminate denominational schools against the interest and expressed desire of the communities they serve would simultaneously breach political principles, violate international conventions, and conflict with existing statutory provisions. In short, it would be unjust and illegal.

What then of the second line of objection; that a religious education is educationally suspect, and a form of indoctrination? No doubt some forms of religious as of other styles of education may involve indoctrination, but unless one insists on regarding every form of imparting any religious beliefs and practices as educationally unacceptable then the case still remains to be made. The mere possibility that religious beliefs may be erroneous no more warrants excluding this dimension of human thought and experience from school than does the possibility that beliefs about art and history may also be mistaken.

Similarly, the claim that by having religion on the schedule other subjects may suffer, is either trivial or question-begging. All timetabling works with limited hours, and proceeds on the basis of resources and perceived priorities. If religion is to be accorded a place, then that restricts the time available for other things; but so too does the provision of a place for any other subject. Every class excludes some other possibility. If the objector responds that time given to religious teaching or worship is necessarily time wasted, because these cannot be truly educational, that only serves to show the question-begging assumption of the argument.

The idea that secular schools can equally respect the religious identities of their pupils rests on a somewhat superficial understanding of religious cultures which regards them as detachable elements. True respect for deep commitments is appropriately marked by permitting communities wishing to educate their children, the means and the environment in which to do so. Certainly a society may reasonably prohibit activities agreed to be injurious but that has no special connection to the issue of church schools – unless, once again, the question of harm and benefit is blatantly begged in favour of secularism.

No argument so far presented has shown that there is anything intrinsically divisive or educationally harmful about Catholic or other denominational schools. On the contrary, consideration of parental and community rights, and the deep connection between religious belief and cultural practice suggests that there are political and educational grounds for favouring them, at least where the needs they serve and the means they employ are not themselves objectionable on other grounds, such as might be relevant to the assessment of any human institution religious or secular.

The principal purpose of Catholic schools is to help implement the duty of Catholic parents to raise their children in the faith, enabling them to lead good and fulfilling lives that will bring them eventually to salvation. In keeping with a long philosophical tradition, the Catholic Church regards the primary responsibility of education in general as residing with parents and family. But in the nature of any major activity in which human beings share a common interest, it makes sense to have a division of labour in order that different forms of expertise will be deployed within organised structures on behalf of the community. Schools come into existence for that purpose. So the function of Catholic schools derives from the duty that attaches to parents to raise their children in the faith, in order that they should, in the words of the *Catechism*, 'come to know, to love and to serve God'.

In considering the *actual* implementation of that role it also has to be recognised that schools have multiple functions. They have to provide children with a basic set of learning skills and with the fundaments of knowledge of sorts that will enable them to acquire further knowledge, and also equip them to understand the society in which they live as well as to prepare themselves for further higher study if they have the aptitude and interest.

Returning to the question of faith it is an essential and ineliminable role for such schools to provide a foundation in religious knowledge and a religious formation: not merely telling people about the content of religious concepts and claims but actually forming them in the light of those ideas and beliefs. Hence there is a clear role for religious instruction designed to enable pupils to develop a religious understanding of their identities as images of God.

Like any other set of educational aims proposed for schools, how well, how fully, and how effectively these are realised within any given institution, or within institutions generally at any given period of time, is going to vary enormously. It will depend in large part upon surrounding cultures: within the local Catholic community, within the Church, and within society more broadly. How well a school can perform will also depend upon the extent of knowledge and support of the parents. Often there is a tendency for people to claim that teachers or schools are not doing a good job while not taking full note of the fact that how well they can discharge their responsibilities depends upon the surrounding context of support, or of the opposition they meet.

Developing patterns of employment: with both parents working, or in some cases no parents working; or single-parent households and so on, have an impact on the expectations of parents, children and teachers regarding the purposes of schooling. In particular there is a growing trend to see schools as providing child-minding services. Then again expectations associated with exam performance, and success in school league tables has an impact on what schools can do. In parallel with these trends, and in part in consequence of them, there has been a marginalisation of the primary function of Catholic schools: to form children so as to help them come to know and to love God. Connected with this is an impoverishment in the knowledge that Catholics possess about the nature of their own faith, and this would include many teachers. Up until the late 1960s the level of catechetical knowledge would have been quite high, certainly much more considerable than it is today. Also the social framework of the parish was very important and that has been weakened.

How reflective such catechetical learning was is another matter, but that is going to be true of any body of knowledge. G. K. Chesterton once observed that part of the trouble with education is that we want to give our children something that we do not ourselves possess. We want them to have a kind of knowledge, a type of virtue, and a degree of commitment that we wish we had ourselves; and we hope that in their case it may not be too late to inculcate these.

Parents sometimes say 'I would like my children to have a grounding in the faith and I expect the school to give it', but if the parents themselves lack this, what reason is there to expect that the teachers who are their own peer group are likely to have it either? It is an improper imposition upon teachers to expect them to carry the entire weight of religious formation. It is also unrealistic because the education the teachers themselves had may not have equipped them for it. It is a dereliction of the responsibility that I identified earlier. The duty of education lies primarily with parents, and in general Catholic schools will only be as good as the communities they serve.

Advocates of Catholic schooling need to ask themselves the question, what are Catholic schools for? and in reflecting upon it remember that their primary function is to discharge on behalf of, and in co-operation with parents the responsibility of raising children to know, to love and to serve God in the Catholic understanding of that knowledge, love and service.

25.

Learning and the mind of God

Jesus said to them 'Therefore I tell you, the kingdom of God will be taken away from you and given to a nation producing the fruits of it' (Matthew 21:43). Holy Scripture is often tough; indeed I cannot think of passages that simply tread water or offer bland affirmation. When God speaks, he calls us to attention, and generally to reform and renewal. Also, what sounds like condemnation is often a warning to relocate one's heart, to shift from false to true goals and values, and to be aware that God and not man is the measure of all things.

One reading of God's authority, of his being the *ruler*, is the familiar moral or legal one. The idea that duty derives from divine commands can be traced back through figures such as Calvin, to the medieval philosopher-theologian William of Ockham, and from there through an Augustinean tradition back to interpretations of scripture, particularly the books of the Old Testament such as Isaiah. But there is another sense in which God may be thought to be a ruler of reality and this is worth mentioning in connection with higher learning. In discussing *truth*, Ockham's near contemporary, Thomas Aquinas, draws on the philosophy of the Greeks filtered through the commentaries of Arabs and Jews. What Aquinas arrives at is the idea that the human intellect is 'measured' by things and that things are 'measured' by God; so that, indirectly, God is the measure of our minds. What he means is that knowledge involves conforming our minds to the structure of reality – grasping the way things are – and that the way things are in the world is a reflection of God's own mind. Our true thoughts are shaped by the world, the world is shaped by God; thus through *science* (in the original broad sense of the term, i.e. organised understanding), we come to know something of the mind of God. Our minds are shaped and measured by the Divine Mind.

This is a profound and inspiring account of knowledge. To some extent it has been rediscovered in writings about contemporary science; for both at the cosmological level and at that of the microphysical, some investigators have come to think of their enquiries as engaging with the mind of God. Recently I took part in a meeting whose theme was one of religion and science. Such an event reflects a wider sense that, far from being hostile to religion, contemporary scientific theories are often congenial to, and indeed may be supportive of, theistic viewpoints.

If we are religious believers this should come as no surprise though it may still be welcome as an overdue return to right reason. What I would urge, however, is that scholars, researchers and students reflect upon Aquinas's account of truth as involving Divine measure, and try to see its implications for their own field of study, *whatever it may be*. For if Aquinas is right we should be able to recover something of the Divine order from each and every aspect of reality. If we also recall the idea that human kind is made in the image of God then study of human existence promises to be especially rewarding and important for discerning Divine purposes. Not only physics, but the other natural sciences, and not only those but the human sciences, and the humanities and the arts, *all* offer scope for communion between the mind of man and the mind of God mediated via *things*.

This vision of human knowledge, both theoretical and practical, as being all of a piece and directed towards God, animated the educational institutions of the Middle Ages from which many existing universities, including my own (St Andrews) inherited much of their form and function.

The term *'universitas'* was just used simply to mean a group of persons united by a common interest or activity. Medieval writers sometimes refer to the Church in the sense of the whole body of Christian believers, in this way. Likewise *'collegium'* simply meant a community and not necessarily an academic one. It is in this sense that we speak of the College of Cardinals in Rome, or of the College of Heralds in London. Each is a community concerned with a common task. The academic use of the term 'college' is then a case of something more general. From the twelfth century there had been a revival of learning in Europe. One of the main influences on this was St Anselm who first integrated the knowledge represented by scripture, ancient philosophy, the Church Fathers and later Christian thinkers. The style and ambition of his work soon lead to a renaissance of education and scholarship. Systematic study such as St Anselm proposed, generated populations of students and masters gathered together in places of study, *studia*.

The next step was to give precise definition and status to these academic communities. This was in part an issue of quality control but there was also a concern to avoid 'duty dodging', for ecclesiastics were permitted to be absent from their churches if they were engaged in study, and many enrolled as students to avoid or delay the regime of the chapel and the cloister. I should add that the move from religious to civic foundations hardly eliminated the motive of work avoidance.

Out of this was born the *Studium Generale*, an academic community of masters and students, membership of which was not restricted by nationality. A true internationalism resulted and was handed on from Church to society. From the thirteenth to the sixteenth centuries and beyond, a network of universities developed stretching from Poland to Scotland, from Italy to Scandinavia. The masters moved to and fro between these carrying old knowledge and new learning, and developing that synthesis of truth and reason which was the culture of the Latin West.

This is the common inheritance of all educated people; but it is that especially of those of us who are members of a university, an institution inspired by this ancient tradition and which seeks to continue it. In an age celebrated for being 'post-modern' and 'multi-cultural', places of traditional learning and value could seem marginal having little to offer the wider world. The truth is *exactly* the opposite of this. What passes for universalism in the contemporary world is largely an ever-expanding, repeating pattern of consumerism, and of media and advertising-driven life styles. Our world may be broader and more rapidly travelled than that of the founders of the ancient universities, but it lacks the cultural unity and spiritual depth of their world. Education then was much more selective and purposeful in its content than is general today.

As I mentioned in connection with Aquinas, the selection was based on Judaeo-Christian assumptions: that the world is created, intelligible, and indicative of its creator; that a covenant was stuck between God and human kind, first with the Jews and later with us all, that the Church and the Scripture it preserves are channels of grace, and that we are called to a supernatural destiny, life with God forever. For a Christian the purposes of education follow directly: to carry us to a proper understanding of what is implied by these assumptions, and to enable us to live and – more importantly – to die well, in the grace of God.

In the contemporary world these views are contested, but more often they are ignored. The enlightenment sought to advance understanding without reference to God or to a purposeful creation. The results are at best uncertain, and I think we may say that the efforts of utopian ideologies to provide heaven without God have been more terrible than the misapplied evangelism (if it were that creditable) of Christians during the crusades against Islam, the persecution of the Jews and the religious wars of Europe. These were profoundly un-Christian deeds. They were sinful, objectively speaking they were

mortally so. Christians should be ashamed of these events;
but they may also feel merit in the fact that perhaps only
Christianity has the resources to express eternal condemnation and sentence upon them.

In Isaiah (5) and then in Matthew (21) we are introduced to the idea of a vineyard, established by a benign
designer, well prepared, and well planted. But the tenants
fail to care for it and in one case produce only sour grapes
and in another attack and kill the owner's son. The threat
of expulsion follows: 'The Kingdom of God will be taken
from you and given to a people who will produce its fruits.'
In one reading the two passages concern the original
covenant: the vineyard is the House of Israel, and what is
forewarned is a turning away of God from his first chosen
people to others who may be more responsive. But there is
another historical and cultural reading which suggests
that unless *we* co-operate with God then what has been
given will be taken away. Who then might *we* be? I have
spoken of the Western tradition of enquiry and education.
This began in Greece, moved in part to the Arab world and
then West so that by the thirteenth century it could be
located in Paris or Cologne; from there it spread throughout Europe and via the European empires to other parts of
the world. No one who works in the universities can fail to
be struck by the thought that in some sense higher-learning has now left the old world and is located in the new –
particularly in the US.

The more important questions to ask are whether the
Christian idea of knowledge as directed towards God has
accompanied higher-learning on its travels, and whether
we in the older universities have been faithful to the vision
of the founders of Western Christian scholarship. The
answers are I think mixed. Of course there are inspiring
Catholic and other Christian scholars in Europe and
America, as well as elsewhere; but the philosophical and
religious ideals associated with traditional conceptions of
knowledge and education have to be rearticulated, and
the institutions of learning reanimated by them if the

vineyards are not to prove barren and the tenants become corrupt. The corrective is provided by Paul's letter to the Philippians (4:8–9):

> Finally brethren, whatever is true, whatever is honourable, whatever is just, whatever is pure, whatever is lovely, whatever is gracious, if there is any excellence, if there is anything worthy of praise, think about these things. What you have learned and received and heard do, and the God of peace will be with you.

Index